CHARLOTTE ADAMS, General Editor
International Cook Book Series

INDONESIAN

COOKERY

by Lie Sek-Hiang

Bonanza Books · New York

This edition published by Bonanza Books,
a division of Crown Publishers, Inc.
C D E F G H

ACKNOWLEDGMENTS

I should like to express my grateful appreciation to the many friends who in one or another way have shown their interest in and taste for Indonesian cooking, and who have encouraged me to write this book.

I should like particularly to mention my indebtedness to Professor M. Sadarjoen, Vice-President, Research Council for Economical, Social and Cultural Affairs (Council for Sciences for Indonesia), Djakarta, Indonesia, and Dr. Warren M. Banner, Director of Research, National Urban League, New York City, for their invaluable assistance throughout.

In getting the book into final form, I owe much to Mrs. Charlotte Adams, who not only edited my manuscript, but gave valuable assistance throughout its preparation.

LIE, SEK-HIANG

New York, 1963

To the memory of my parents
To my brothers and sisters

 # CONTENTS

INTRODUCTION

Indonesia is a melting pot of many nations, each of which has influenced the culture of the country to some degree. To understand and appreciate Indonesian food, it is important to have some idea of these influences, as well as the geography and history of the country.

Briefly, the Republic of Indonesia, a lush, volcanic land, is an island nation, consisting of six main groups and more than 3,000 smaller islands. The total land area is about 735,000 square miles, roughly three times the size of Texas. Indonesia comprises the greatest agglomeration of islands to form a single country anywhere in the world. The largest of these islands are Sumatra, Kalimantan (Borneo), Sulawesi (Celebes), Java, Madura, Bali, and Irian Barat (West Irian). Bali is best known to Westerners.

By the end of 1963 it is expected that the population of Indonesia will have reached 100,000,000. At present, 70 per cent of the total population lives on the island of Java.

Historical records of Indonesia begin with the invasion of Hindu and Buddhist influences from India. The cultural heritage of that period is still preserved in the life and art of Bali, whose people remain Hindus. Islam, the faith of Mohammed, was brought to Indonesia by Arab and Indian Moslem traders, and by the latter half of the sixteenth century, when the Portuguese reached the islands, was well established on Sumatra and Java. The British and the Dutch, interested like the Portuguese in the spice trade, followed, and before long the Dutch drove the English and Portuguese from the islands. For 350 years Indonesia was a Dutch colony, but in 1945 the liberation leader,

Sukarno, proclaimed Indonesia's independence, and now very few Dutch remain in the country. The Chinese, however, have been settling in Indonesia, in large numbers, since the eighteenth century, and have maintained their own culture, which has had considerable influence on the food and cooking of their adopted country.

And now to the food itself! In the United States and Europe I have taught housewives to cook Indonesian dishes. They have not had difficulty in learning, and they have enjoyed the experience, appreciating the unique flavors, attractive appearance, and nutritive values of the dishes. This is why I have written this book, and I hope I have made it of practical use to Westerners. I also hope that it will be of aid and interest to persons who already know and love Indonesian food but have thus far had no instructions for preparing it.

The recipes included here are traditional, and many of them date back for generations. The fact, however, that they are presented in book form is unorthodox, as they have usually been handed down by word of mouth or by observation of one generation by the next. The recipes comprise all those which are well known, from every part of Indonesia, selected from the thousands of regional specialties available. I have chosen those that I find appeal most to Western taste.

Chinese food is popular in Indonesia, and many basically Chinese ingredients have become an inherent part of Indonesian cuisine. Preparation of vegetable dishes in Indonesia has been adopted from the Chinese way of cooking: vegetables are stir-fried, briefly, to retain the bright color and crisp texture. Indonesians, like the Chinese, are noted for the low fat content of their dishes, a matter of great interest in the West today.

If you are familiar with the Dutch, Indian, and Arab cuisines, you will perhaps recognize the influence they have had on Indonesian cooking. However, I have eliminated all dishes frequently served in Indonesia but deriving entirely from other countries. In other words, every dish presented here is *primarily* Indonesian.

The various parts of Indonesia express their own local characteristics, not only in their language, art, dance, and culture, but also in their food. For example, Sumatrans are active, openhearted and quick. Their food is always substantial. They eat lots of meat, including buffalo, and great use of hot red pepper and turmeric gives their food a yellowish-red color. In contrast, the Javanese are sober and rather quiet. While they also use spices in their food, it is, in addition, much sweeter than the Sumatran. And so it goes, through all 3,000 islands!

Many people believe that all Indonesian food is hotly spiced. This is not necessarily true. Lots of Indonesians do not like highly seasoned food. Therefore, as in many other cuisines, the food is seasoned to fit individual or family tastes. There are dishes in which a great deal of hot pepper can be used, but the pepper is usually served separately so everyone may take as much or as little as he likes.

For breakfast Indonesians drink the famous Java coffee, with bread and eggs if they can afford them. Those who cannot accompany their coffee with boiled cassava roots, fried or boiled sweet potatoes, and steamed bananas. Lunch and dinner are both rice tables, and both are customarily taken in the home.

The working day begins at seven-thirty in the morning, due to the unbearable heat characteristic of this tropical country. At two everybody goes home for luncheon, which is followed by a siesta. Thus all offices and shops are closed from two to four in the afternoon. Between five and six in the afternoon, Java tea is served with various tea delicacies, some of which appear in this book. Dinner is served late, as is the case in most siesta-taking countries.

In general, Indonesian women are good cooks, and they spend several hours a day preparing food for their families.

Preparation techniques are different from those used in the West. For example, as in most of the Oriental countries, meat is cut into small pieces, sliced, or cubed so that it may absorb flavor from the spices used with it. Seasoning is done both before and during the cooking.

In preparing this book, I have endeavored to make everything as easy and simple for you as possible. If certain ingredients are not likely to be available in the United States, substitutes are suggested. You will find definitions and descriptions of Indonesian ingredients and a list of places where they can be bought. Names of dishes are given in English, then in Indonesian. In cases where the same dish has different names in different parts of the Republic, all those names are given. I have also provided some sample rice-table menus, just to start you off on planning your own.

In the recipes, the ingredients that are marked with an asterisk (*) are those not familiar to American cooks. An explanation of these ingredients can be found in Chapter 2: Indonesian Ingredients.

I am delighted to present this book to my many Western friends, and I do hope that these recipes will open up a new world of flavors to American tables and add considerably to the delights of many homes.

CHAPTER 1

THE INDONESIAN RICE TABLE

The rice table is a unique Indonesian way of eating. It may be produced at lunch or dinner, or both, and consists of rice served with a number of other dishes. In Indonesian hotels, two plates are placed on the table for each person. Then a series of boys arrives, each carrying rice or one of the other dishes presented to accompany it. The guest places rice on one plate, then takes what he wishes from the other dishes, putting them on or around the rice and also on the second plate. This way of serving might make you think at once that the whole idea is beyond a servantless American home. But it should be evident to you at once that such a meal can be served on a buffet table, with success and a flourish!

The other dishes served with the rice are varied and fascinating. They comprise meat, fish, vegetables, hot and sweet relishes, crisp and soft fritters, and many more. The contrasts are exciting—spicy and bland, hot and cold, crisp and soft, sweet and sour. In planning a rice table, consideration must be taken to bring in all these factors, in large or small quantity. Sometimes there are four dishes, sometimes forty. The cardinal rule is that flavors should not be repeated, so that careful planning is required to make a truly varied and interesting rice table.

A small rice table can serve four to six people, but can be increased to serve ten or fifteen with relatively little extra work. It consists usually of one meat or poultry dish, one fish, one vegetable, one salad, one sweet or sour relish, one hot relish, and one kind of fritter. If you add one more dish, the whole will serve at least two more people. The large rice table of forty dishes can serve a hundred.

Most of the meat, fish, and poultry dishes can be prepared a few days ahead and kept in the refrigerator, They taste better when stored at least overnight because the foods will absorb the spices more thoroughly. Vegetables, on the other hand, should be prepared just before serving.

Dessert at a rice table is usually a variety of fruits. The fruits available in Indonesia are incredible: enormous oranges whose colors range from flame to dark green; mandarins, large and small, and also varied in color; grapefruit; mangoes of more than ten varieties of color, taste, and shape; several kinds of bananas; pineapples and papayas; avocados; and specifically Indonesian fruits like sawos, rambutans, dukus, tjempedak, mangistans, nangkas, and durians! You haven't all of these in the West, but enough fruits are available to you to make a handsome display and give a good variety of texture and flavor.

Another factor about the rice table that makes it perfect for a buffet party is that it is eaten with a spoon and fork. Knives are never necessary, which should be true of all buffet food.

Just imagine how handsome and appetizing a large number of these dishes will look when you place them on a buffet table. My Western friends who have enjoyed Indonesian food this way at my home are very enthusiastic about it. I hope you will be too!

CHAPTER 2

INDONESIAN INGREDIENTS

ABALONES: Two varieties are available, dried
(*pauhi*) ones and others in cans. Since the dried ones can be bought only in Chinese grocery stores, it is easier to use the canned ones.

AGAR-AGAR: A gelatinous substance derived from seaweed. Sold by the ounce in Chinese and Japanese grocery stores.

BAMBOO SHOOTS: Two varieties are available, salted
(*rebung*) and unsalted. Both come in cans. The unsalted are the ones usually used in Indonesian dishes. They can be found in big grocery stores.

BEAN CAKE: Sold in square cakes in Chinese and
(*tahu*) Japanese grocery stores. Those from the Chinese are harder and more compact than the Japanese ones.

BEAN SPROUTS: Two types of bean sprouts are sold
(*tauge, toge*) in Chinese and Japanese grocery
stores, soybean sprouts and mung-
bean sprouts. Indonesian dishes use
the familiar type—that is, the mung-
bean sprouts—although the Chinese
prefer the soybean sprouts, which
have a stronger flavor and crunchier
texture. Mung-bean sprouts are sold,
canned, in supermarkets.

BIRD'S-NEST: A gelatinous material coating the
(*sarang burung*) nests of sea swallows. These birds
build their nests among the cliffs
and in sea caves. The nests are
picked, soaked in water, cleaned,
and dried. Used mostly for soups,
they are sold in Chinese grocery
stores in boxes.

BITTER MELON: Available only in Chinese grocery
(*pare-pare*) stores and sold by the pound. This
melon has a cool and slightly bitter
taste.

CELLOPHANE NOODLES: *See* SHINING NOODLES

CHINESE LEEK: Sold by the pound in Chinese gro-
(*kutjai*) cery stores. Because of its flavor,
used in many dishes. Usually kept in
the refrigerator.

CHINESE MUSHROOMS: Dried brown-colored mushrooms
(*djamur kering*) with black caps. They come in different sizes and are sold in Chinese
and Japanese grocery stores.

CHINESE NOODLES: Available in Chinese grocery stores
(*misoa*) and sold by the pound.

CHINESE SAUSAGES: Available in Chinese grocery stores.
(laktjang)

CHINESE SCALLION: A small green plant with an onion-like odor. Sold in Chinese grocery stores. The delicate flavor is very suitable for seasoning fish and meat dishes.
(daon bawang)

CLOUD EARS: A cultivated tree fungus available in Chinese and Japanese grocery stores.
(djamur kuping)

COCONUT: Coconut is eaten in many forms. Coconut milk or cream from coconut is made from grated fresh or dried coconut mixed with water and squeezed through a cloth or strainer. It is used in food.
(kelapa)
COCONUT MILK:
(santan)

CORIANDER: A herb of the parsley family, grown for its aromatic seeds. Used for flavoring pickles, curries, and other food, it is available in local markets.
(ketumbar)

CUMIN: An aromatic seed, used for flavoring food. Available in local markets.
(djintan)

CURRY POWDER: A blend of highly spiced condiments used for seasoning food. Available in local markets.
(kerie)

DRIED CABBAGE: Salted and dried and sold by the ounce in Chinese grocery stores. Used for soups and steamed dishes.
(tongtjay)

DRIED NOODLES: Noodles in Chinese grocery stores are sold fresh or in dried form. The dried noodles come in different varieties.
(mie kering)

EGG ROLL WRAPPERS: Sold in Chinese grocery stores by
(*kulit lumpia*) the pound, each pound containing
24 wrappers. Each egg roll wrapper,
cut in four square pieces, can be
used for wonton wrappers. (Egg roll
wrappers may also be made in the
home. See recipe for Fried Egg Roll
[p. 227]).

FISH, DRIED: Available in Chinese and Japanese
(*ikan kering*) grocery stores and in local markets.
They come in different varieties,
salted and unsalted.

GINGER (ROOT): Sold by the pound in Chinese and
(*djahe*) Japanese grocery stores and some
supermarkets, and used as a condiment in foods. (*See also* Sliced
Ginger, p. 234).

GLUTINOUS
or STICKY RICE: Sold by the pound in Chinese gro-
(*ketan, beras ketan*) cery stores.

GLUTINOUS RICE FLOUR: Sold by the pound in Chinese gro-
(*tepung beras ketan*) cery stores.

GOLDEN NEEDLES: *See* TIGER LILIES

HAM: The kind most resembling the native
product is Smithfield.

HOT GREEN PEPPERS: *See* PEPPERS.

HOT RED PEPPERS: *See* PEPPERS.

HOT SAUCE: Made from ground hot red pepper
(*sambal*) mixed with lemon juice. Can be replaced with tabasco sauce, sold in
grocery stores.

MUNG BEANS:
(*katjang hidjau*) Sold by the pound in Chinese and Japanese grocery stores, they are used for growing bean sprouts and for making bean flour.

MUSTARD GREENS, SALTED:
(*sajur asin*) Available in Chinese grocery stores. Sold in jars or small cans.

OYSTER SAUCE:
(*saos tiram*) Sold in bottles in Chinese grocery stores and used as a condiment. *Not* interchangeable with soy sauce.

PEPPERS, HOT RED
and **HOT GREEN**
(capsicum family—**CHILI,**
BIRD, TOBASCO): Capsicums vary in color, size, form,

(*lombok, lada mudah,*
tjabe, tjabe rawit, lada,
lada burung) and flavor, from very hot to sweetly pungent. They are used as a condiment or as a vegetable, or both.

RICE FLOUR:
(*tepung beras*) Sold by the pound in Chinese grocery stores.

RICE STICKS:
(*bihun*) Made from cooked rice and dried, they are sold by the pound in Chinese grocery stores.

SHARK'S FINS:
(*haaievin, sirip*
ikan hui) Sold dry, in sheets, in Chinese grocery stores. Used for soups, they are rather expensive.

SHINING
or **CELLOPHANE NOODLES:**
(*so-un, laksa*) Made from boiled rice and sold by the pound in Chinese and Japanese grocery stores.

SHRIMP, DRIED: Sold by the pound in Chinese and
(*udang kering, ebbi*) Japanese grocery stores.

SHRIMP PASTE, SALTED: Used as a condiment and available
(*terasi*) in Chinese and Japanese grocery
stores. Sold in jars imported from
the Philippines and Indonesia.

SHRIMP PUFFS, CHIPS,
or **WAFERS:** Originally made in Indonesia from
(*krupuk*) tapioca flour mixed with fish or
shrimp and spices. Now made locally
and sold in Chinese grocery stores.

SHRIMP SAUCE: A black sauce made from shrimp or
(*petis, patis*) fish, used for salad dressing or on
cold food. Available in Chinese and
Japanese grocery stores and sold in
jars imported from the Philippines
and Indonesia.

SNOW PEAS: Sold fresh, by the pound, in Chinese
(*katjang kapri*) grocery stores, these have a very delicate texture and subtle taste. Usu-
ally kept in the refrigerator.

SOYBEANS: Sold by the pound in Chinese and
(*katjang kedele*) Japanese grocery stores, they are
used for making bean sprouts, salted
soybeans, soy sauce, and bean cakes.

SOYBEANS, SALTED: Made from soybeans and sold in
(*taotjo*) cans in Chinese and Japanese grocery stores. Used as a condiment.

SQUID, DRIED: Sold by the pound in Chinese and
(*djuhi*) Japanese grocery stores.

TAMARIND: Fruit of a tropical tree used as a
(*asam*) condiment. It has a sour taste and
can be replaced with lemon juice.
Available in Chinese and Spanish-
American grocery stores. (*See also*
Tamarind Juice, p. 235.)

TIGER LILIES:
or **GOLDEN NEEDLES:** Dried lily flowers of a gold color.
(*sedap malam*) They possess nutritive values and
are cooked with meat, poultry, and
vegetables. Sold by the ounce in
Chinese grocery stores.

TURMERIC: An aromatic root used as a condi-
(*kunit*) ment. Available in powder form in
local markets.

WATER CHESTNUTS: Sold in cans in Chinese and Japa-
(*berangan*) nese grocery stores and used as a
vegetable.

WHITE RADISH, SALTED: Sold by the pound in Chinese gro-
(*lobak asin*) cery stores.

WONTON SKINS: Available by the pound in Chinese
(*kulit pangsit*) grocery stores. One-half pound gives
about 40 wontons. *See also* EGG ROLL
WRAPPERS.

CHAPTER 3

SOURCES FOR INDONESIAN INGREDIENTS

Most of the ingredients mentioned in the various recipes of this book are available in local Chinese and Japanese grocery stores. Some may even be found in your regular supermarket.

If you are unable to find what you need in your local area, write to any of the following shops, which will be glad to fill mail orders.

EASTERN TRADING COMPANY
(Mrs. Chang)
2801 Broadway
(corner 108th Street,
Columbia University
vicinity)
New York 25, N. Y.
Telephone:
MOnument 6-6644
Cable Address: Eastrako

A BIT OF BALI
(Indonesian restaurant)
127 West 43rd Street
New York 36, N. Y.

YUIT HING MARKET
CORPORATION
23 Pell Street
New York 13, N. Y.

CHONG LUNG
18 Hudson Street
Boston 11, Mass.

T. H. LUNG
9 Hudson Street
Boston 11, Mass.

WING SING CHONG COMPANY
1076 Stockton Street
San Francisco, Calif.

TUCK CHEONG AND COMPANY
617 H Street N. W.
Washington, D. C.

YEE SING CHONG COMPANY
950 Castelar Street
Los Angeles, Calif.

MEE YUN MERCANTILE
  COMPANY
2223 Wentworth Avenue
Chicago. Ill.

SUN WAH HING TRADING
  COMPANY
2246 Wentworth Avenue
Chicago, Ill.

LUN YICK COMPANY
1339 Third Avenue
Detroit, Mich.

SUN LEE YUEN COMPANY
1726 Payne Avenue
Cleveland, Ohio

YICK FUNG COMPANY
210 North Ninth Street
Philadelphia, Pa.

MRS. DEWILDT*
4-B Lakeview Drive
Kinnelon, N. J.
Telephone: 838-3990,
  Area Code 201

* This shop has imported a large collection of authentic ingredients and
preserved condiments. A price list is available.

CHAPTER 4

✿✿✿ SAMPLE MENUS FOR THE RICE TABLE

FOR 2 PERSONS

Fried rice
Shrimp puffs
Sweet-and-sour radish relish
Hot shrimp relish

✿

Boiled rice
Boiled chicken with soy sauce
Omelet with coconut milk
Sautéed green beans
Hot fish relish
Pineapple fritters

✿

Boiled rice
Shrimp with Chinese mushrooms
Chicken liver sambal goreng
Sweet-and-sour cucumber relish
Hot shrimp-paste relish

✿

❦

Boiled rice
Fried fish
Braised beef with soy sauce
Crisp fritters with dried shrimp
Fried hot relish with peanuts
Pickled mixed vegetable relish with turmeric

❦

FOR 4–6 PERSONS

Boiled rice
Shrimp with tomato sauce
Braised beef with ginger
Sautéed bamboo shoots
Shrimp puffs
Hot fish relish
Pickled mixed vegetable relish

❦

Boiled rice
Sweet-and-sour shrimp
Stewed beef with broth
Sambal goreng tahu
Sweet-and-sour radish relish
Hot shrimp-paste relish
Banana fritters

❦

Boiled rice
Broiled chicken with soy sauce
Omelet with coconut milk
Sautéed bean sprouts
Sweet-and-sour bamboo shoots
Pineapple fritters
Hot peanut relish

❦

Fried rice
Potato chips with red pepper
Pickled cucumber relish
Shrimp puffs
Hot tomato relish

FOR 8–15 PERSONS

Boiled rice
Fish with fresh mushrooms
Sautéed pork liver
Beef on skewers with spices
Eggplant with coconut milk
Hot coconut relish
Pickled mixed vegetable relish
Crisp dried shrimp fritters

Boiled rice
Chicken soup
Shrimp with fresh asparagus
Pork with soy sauce
Braised beef Balinese style
Hot soybean relish
Sweet pineapple relish
Banana fritters

Boiled rice
Crisp noodle dish
Fried shrimp balls
Pork with soy sauce and potatoes
Braised beef with spices
Mixed salad, style I
Crisp peanut fritters
Hot dried fish relish
Sweet-and-sour white radish relish

꿮

Boiled rice
Noodle dish, Javanese style
Cucumber soup
Shrimp with snow peas
Barbecued pork
Braised beef in butter sauce
Sautéed bamboo shoots
Hot green pepper relish
Pickled cucumber relish
Shrimp puffs

꿮

CHAPTER 5

RICE DISHES

BOILED RICE

Nasi

In Indonesia rice is steamed, not boiled, and perhaps you will prefer to cook it that way. Indonesians do it in a steamer consisting of a copper pot (*dandang*) and a bamboo container (*kukusan*). It is not true, as you may have heard, that Indonesians cook their rice a day in advance in order to get it dry. Since there is almost no refrigeration, rice would spoil overnight in Indonesia's hot and humid climate. It is steaming that makes our rice dry. It is possible, however, to get dry rice by boiling, so here I have given you recipes for that method.

For rice dishes, servings for men are larger than for women. One cup of rice when cooked will be enough to serve three men, while one half of this amount is usually enough to serve three women. One cup of raw rice makes two cups, cooked.

To cook soft rice, use two cups of water to a cup of rice. For hard rice, such as is used for fried rice, use a cup and a half of water to one cup of rice. Using this quantity guide, add water to rice and bring to a boil. Turn heat low, cover tightly, and cook 20 minutes.

Never stir the rice. If you cook a larger quantity than one cup at a time, the rice may take longer to cook. The rice on top should be flaky and cooked through. If the rice is done, a grain can be easily mashed with the fingers. Either short-grain or long-grain rice is suitable for Indonesian dishes.

FRIED RICE

Nasi Goreng

6 servings

4 cups boiled rice
6 medium eggs
4 tablespoons vegetable oil
2 medium onions, minced
1 clove garlic, minced
½ cup minced pork or bacon
½ cup shrimp, shelled and cooked
2 tablespoons soy sauce
salt and pepper to taste
2 hot red peppers, sliced thin (*optional*)*
½ cup Smithfield ham, cut in strips 1 inch long by ⅛ inch wide
½ cup crabmeat
¼ cup chopped celery
½ cup fried crisp onion flakes (*see index*)

Beat eggs. Heat a skillet and grease it with a few drops of oil. Make 4 thin omelets (*see index*). Place aside to be used as garnish. Add 2 tablespoons oil to skillet, heat, and make thicker omelet from rest of eggs, cutting in ½-inch-square pieces.

Fry onion and garlic in 2 tablespoons of oil for 2 minutes. Add minced pork, stirring until pork is done. Add shrimp, omelet pieces, soy sauce, salt, pepper, and rice, then mix together on low heat for about 10 minutes.

Garnish with sliced omelets, red peppers, ham, crabmeat, celery, and onion flakes.

FRIED RICE, JAVANESE STYLE

Nasi Goreng Djawa

6 servings

4 cups boiled rice
6 medium eggs
4 tablespoons vegetable oil
2 medium onions, minced
1 clove garlic, minced
½ cup ground dried shrimp*
½ cup minced beef
2 tablespoons soy sauce
2 hot red peppers, sliced thin (*optional*)*
salt and pepper to taste
1 medium cucumber, sliced
½ cup fried crisp onion flakes (*see index*)

Beat eggs. Heat a skillet and grease it with a few drops of oil. Make 4 thin omelets (*see index*). Place aside to be used as garnish. Add about 2 tablespoons oil to skillet, heat, and make thicker omelet from rest of egg. Remove, cut in ½-inch-square pieces. Heat skillet, add rest of oil to skillet, heat, and fry onions and garlic for 2 minutes. Add beef, stir until beef is well done. Add shrimp, omelet pieces, soy sauce, salt, pepper, red peppers, and rice. Mix together on a low heat for about 8 minutes.

Garnish with sliced omelets, sliced cucumber, and crisp onion flakes.

RICE DISH I

Nasi Uduk, Nasi Langi

6 servings

2 cups raw rice
4 tablespoons vegetable oil
1 medium onion, minced
2 cloves garlic, minced
4 cups coconut milk*
  salt and pepper to taste
1 teaspoon ground coriander
1 teaspoon ground caraway
2 bay leaves
1 cup canned corned beef
6 medium eggs
½ cup fried crisp onion flakes (*see index*)
2 hot red peppers, sliced thin (*optional*)
1 medium cucumber, sliced thin
½ cup fried soybeans (*see index*)
¼ cup ground dried shrimp*

Heat oil, brown onion and garlic. Add coconut milk, salt, pepper, coriander, caraway, bay leaves, and rice. Bring to a boil, turn heat low. Cook 30–40 minutes, or until rice is done. Cook corned beef in an ungreased frying pan until crisp. Beat eggs and fry thin omelets (*see index*). Cook dried shrimp in an ungreased skillet until crisp. Garnish rice with sliced omelet, corned beef, dried shrimp, onion flakes, red peppers, cucumber, and soybeans.

Variation 1: RICE DISH II

Nasi Guri

6 servings

Follow same procedure as in Rice Dish I, but add to garnish ½ cup coarsely ground peanuts and 10 mint leaves.

Variation 2: RICE DISH WEST JAVANESE STYLE

Nasi Ulam

> *6 servings*

Follow same procedure as in Rice Dish I, but substitute following garnish:

> ½ cup fried soybeans (*see index*)
> ½ cup fried dried fish, crushed°
> 1 medium cucumber, sliced
>   hot shrimp-paste relish (*see index*)
> 10 mint leaves (*optional*)

YELLOW RICE

Nasi Kuning

> *6 servings*

> 2 cups rice
> 4 cups coconut milk°
> 1 medium onion, minced
> 1 tablespoon turmeric°
>   salt and pepper to taste
> 4 medium eggs
> ½ cup canned corned beef
> 2 hot red peppers, sliced (*optional*)°
> 1 medium cucumber, sliced
> ½ cup fried crisp onion flakes (*see index*)

Mix coconut milk with onion, turmeric, salt, pepper, and rice. Cook 20–40 minutes, or until rice is done. Beat eggs and fry thin omelets (*see index*). Cook corned beef in an ungreased pan until crisp. Garnish rice with sliced omelet, red pepper, cucumber, corned beef, and onion flakes.

SPICED RICE
Nasi Kebuli

6 servings

2 cups rice
2 medium onions, minced
3 cloves garlic, minced
½ cup butter (1 stick)
2 cups water
2 cups milk
salt and pepper to taste
10 whole cloves
4 2-inch pieces cinnamon stick
5 cardamon seeds, crushed
1 nutmeg, cut in quarters
4 medium eggs

Brown onions and garlic in the butter. Add water, milk, rice, salt, and other spices. Bring to a boil. Reduce heat, cover tightly, and cook 20–40 minutes, or until rice is done. Beat eggs and fry thin omelets (*see index*). Garnish rice with sliced omelet and serve with the following dishes: Braised Beef with Spices (Gulai Bagar) (*see index*) and Sweet Pineapple Relish (Petjili Nanas) (*see index*).

YELLOW GLUTINOUS RICE
Nasi Kuning Ketan

6 servings

1½ cups glutinous rice*
1 tablespoon turmeric*
1 tablespoon lemon juice
3 cups coconut milk*
salt to taste

1 medium onion, minced
4 medium eggs
1 medium cucumber, sliced

Cover rice with water. Add turmeric and lemon juice; soak overnight. (The lemon juice will give brightness to the color.) Drain rice. Cook in coconut milk, with onion and salt, for 20–40 minutes, or until rice is done. Beat eggs and fry thin omelets (*see index*). Garnish rice with sliced omelet and cucumber. Serve with the following dishes: Broiled Chicken with Coconut Milk (Ajam Panggang Santan) (*see index*) or Beef with Coconut Milk (Gulai Kelio) (*see index*).

RICE COOKED IN CHEESE CLOTH BAGS

Lontong

6 servings

The lontong is rice cooked in banana leaves folded in the form of a sausage. Where banana leaves cannot be obtained, replace with cheese cloth bags, 6 inches long and 1½ inches in diameter.

Fill bags ⅔ full of rice, sew up, and cook in boiling water for about 2 hours. For 6 bags used 2¼ cups rice. When the rice is done remove from bags, cut in ½-inch slices and serve with Charcoal-Grilled Meat on Skewers (Sates) (*see index*) and Green Beans with Coconut Milk (Sajor Sambal Buntjies) (*see index*).

RICE PORRIDGE
Bubur Nasi

2 *servings*

½ cup rice
2 cups water
salt to taste

Bring rice, water, and salt to a boil. Reduce heat and boil for about 20 minutes, or until rice is soft. During cooking, stir 2 or 3 times. More water can be added if desired. This porridge can be served with various dishes.

RICE PORRIDGE WITH COCONUT MILK
Bubur Santan

2 *servings*

½ cup rice
2 cups coconut milk*
salt to taste

Bring rice, coconut milk, and salt to a boil. Reduce heat and cook for about 20 minutes. During cooking, stir 2 or 3 times. This porridge can be served with various dishes.

PORRIDGE SERVED ON ASJURA[1]
Bubur Asjura

6 *servings*

¼ cup peanuts
¼ cup soybeans*
¼ cup red kidney beans

[1] Asjura is a Mohammedan holiday.

¼ cup white kidney beans
1 cup rice
6 cups water
   salt and pepper to taste
2 medium eggs

Cover beans with water and soak for 24 hours. Drain. Bring water and rice to a boil, add peanuts and beans. Reduce heat and cook for 30–40 minutes, or until beans and rice are soft. Stir 2 or 3 times during cooking. Beat eggs and fry thin omelets (*see index*). Garnish rice and beans with sliced omelet. Can be served with various dishes.

PORRIDGE MENADONESE STYLE[1]

Bubur Tinotuan

6 servings

5 cups water
1 cup rice
½ cup corn
½ cup diced sweet potatoes
2 bay leaves
   salt to taste

Bring water, rice, corn, sweet potatoes, bay leaves, and salt to a boil. Turn heat low and cook for about 30–40 minutes, or until rice is soft. Stir 2 or 3 times during cooking.

Serve with Fried Fish (Ikan Goreng) (*see index*) and Tomatoes with Coconut Milk (Masak Tomat) (*see index*).

[1] Menado is a city on the isle of Celebes.

RICE PORRIDGE WITH CHICKEN

Bubur Ajam

6 servings

1 chicken breast
6 cups water
1 medium onion, sliced
1 tablespoon vegetable oil
2 tablespoons dried shrimp*
½ cup salted dried cabbage*
1 tablespoon soy sauce
1 cup rice
   salt and pepper to taste
½ cup chopped celery
½ cup fried crisp onion flakes (*see index*)

Cook chicken in the water, over low heat, for 20 minutes. Remove chicken, save stock. Cut chicken in very thin slices. Brown sliced onion and garlic in oil, then add dried shrimp, chicken, cabbage, soy sauce, rice, chicken stock, salt, and pepper. Cook for about 30–40 minutes, or until rice is soft. Stir 2 or 3 times during cooking. Garnish with chopped celery and onion flakes. Serve hot.

Variation 1: *RICE PORRIDGE WITH PORK*

Bubur Babi

6 servings

In the above, substitute ½ pound ground pork for the chicken.

Variation 2: *RICE PORRIDGE WITH OYSTERS*

Bubur Tiram

6 servings

Add ½ cup of oysters or clams to the Rice Porridge with Pork, above. When using dried oysters, soak 12 hours before adding to the rice mixture.

CHAPTER 6

NOODLE DISHES

NOODLE DISH JAVANESE STYLE

Mie Djawa

6 servings

½ pound dried noodles*
1 medium onion, minced
3 cloves garlic, minced
1 tablespoon vegetable oil
2 stalks Chinese scallion, sliced*
½ cup chopped beef
2 tablespoons soy sauce
1 cup shredded white cabbage
3 medium eggs
½ cup fried crisp onion flakes (see index)
2 cups shrimp puffs (see index)

Cook noodles in boiling water 5 minutes, rinse with cold water, and drain. Brown onion and garlic in oil, then add scallion, beef, soy sauce, and cabbage and cook 10 minutes. Add noodles, mix carefully, and simmer 5 minutes more. Beat eggs and fry thin omelets (see index).

Garnish noodle mixture with sliced omelet, onion flakes, and shrimp puffs.

CRISP NOODLE DISH

Ifu Mie Tjha

6 servings

½ pound dried noodles*
½ cup vegetable oil
2 medium onions, minced
3 cloves garlic, minced
¼ cup shredded chicken
¼ cup sliced pork
¼ cup shrimp, shelled and cooked
2 tablespoons soy sauce
    salt and pepper to taste
3 cups chicken or pork stock
1 cup sliced cauliflower
½ cup Smithfield ham, cut in strips 1 inch long by
    ⅛ inch wide
¼ cup chopped celery
½ cup fried crisp onion flakes (see index)

Put noodles in boiling water and cook for 5 minutes. Rinse with cold water and drain. Heat oil and fry noodles, a few at a time, until light brown and crisp. Remove most of oil, leaving 1 tablespoon in pan. Brown minced onion and garlic, and add chicken, pork, shrimp, soy sauce, salt, pepper, and stock. Simmer for 10 minutes. Add cauliflower and remove from heat. Place a handful of noodles on each plate, add sauce mixture, and garnish with sliced ham, celery, and onion flakes. Serve immediately.

Note: Noodles, already fried, can be bought in grocery stores in tins or boxes.

Variation 1: LONGEVITY NOODLES

Mie Pandjang Umur

6 servings

Follow the same procedure as in Crisp Noodle Dish, but do not fry noodles. Cook noodles in boiling water 5 minutes, rinse with cold water, and drain. Using cups instead of plates, place 2 tablespoons noodles in each, pour sauce mixture over, and garnish with ham, celery, and onion flakes. Serve hot.

Variation 2: FRIED NOODLES

Mie Goreng

6 servings

Use the same ingredients as for Crisp Noodle Dish, but use only ½ cup chicken stock and ¼ cup vegetable oil. Cook noodles in boiling water for 5 minutes, rinse with cold water, and drain. Fry all other ingredients in oil for 10 minutes. Add noodles and stock, stir 5 minutes. Garnish with ham, celery, and onion flakes, and serve.

NOODLE SOUP WITH WONTON

Mie Pangsit

6 servings

½ pound dried noodles*
1 medium onion, minced
2 cloves garlic, minced
1 tablespoon vegetable oil
½ cup shredded chicken
2 tablespoons soy sauce
2 stalks Chinese scallion, minced*
   salt and pepper to taste
4 cups chicken stock
12 fried wonton (*see index*)
½ cup Smithfield ham, cut in strips 1 inch long
   by ⅛ inch wide
½ cup fried crisp onion flakes (*see index*)

Cook noodles in boiling water 5 minutes, rinse with cold water, and drain. Brown onion and garlic in oil, then add chicken, soy sauce, scallion, salt, pepper, and chicken stock. Simmer 5 minutes, then add noodles. Put 2 wontons in each cup, and pour noodle mixture over. Garnish with ham and onion flakes and serve.

NOODLE SOUP WITH TRIPE

Soto Mie

6 servings

1 pound beef tripe
1 medium onion, minced
2 cloves garlic, minced
1 tablespoon vegetable oil
3 slices ginger, 1 inch long by ⅛ inch wide
   (*see index*)
   salt and pepper to taste
½ pound dried noodles*
1 pound bean sprouts*
½ cup chopped celery
½ cup fried crisp onion flakes (*see index*)
2 tablespoons crushed hot red peppers*
3 tablespoons lemon juice

Cut tripe in strips 1½ inches long by ½ inch wide. Cook in boiling water 5 minutes and drain. Brown onion and garlic in oil, add ginger, salt, pepper, and tripe. Cover with water and cook on low heat 1½ hours, or until tripe is tender.

Cook noodles in boiling water 5 minutes, rinse in cold water, and drain. Two minutes before serving, add noodles and bean sprouts to tripe. Garnish with celery and onion flakes.

Mix hot red pepper with lemon juice and serve this mixture, with soy sauce, on the side.

SAUTÉED RICE STICKS

Bihun Goreng

6 servings

2 medium onions, minced
3 cloves garlic, minced
2 tablespoons vegetable oil
½ cup sliced pork
½ cup shredded chicken
½ cup shelled shrimp
2 tablespoons soy sauce
1 cup shredded white cabbage
2 stalks Chinese scallion, sliced*
2 cups chicken stock
½ pound rice sticks*
1 pound bean sprouts*
½ cup fried crisp onion flakes (*see index*)
½ cup chopped celery
½ cup Smithfield ham, cut in strips 1 inch long
    by ½ inch wide

Brown onion and garlic in oil, then add pork, chicken, shrimp, soy sauce, cabbage, scallion, and stock. Simmer 5 minutes. Wash rice sticks quickly, drain, and add to sauce mixture. Mix carefully and cook for 8 minutes. Two minutes before serving, add bean sprouts, constantly stirring to prevent burning. Garnish with onion flakes, celery, and ham.

Variation: RICE STICKS WITH BROTH

Bihun Kuah

6 servings

Follow the same procedure as in Sautéed Rice Sticks, but add 3 cups of stock to ingredients.

RICE STICKS WITH COCONUT MILK
Laksa

6 servings

1 medium onion, minced
2 cloves garlic, minced
2 tablespoons vegetable oil
2 tablespoons turmeric*
1 teaspoon ground ginger
1 teaspoon paprika
4 cups coconut milk*
1 teaspoon ground coriander
1 teaspoon ground caraway
   salt to taste
½ pound rice sticks
4 large hard-cooked eggs, chopped
10 fresh mint leaves (*optional*)
1 cup shredded chicken
½ cup shrimp, shelled and cooked

Brown onion and garlic in oil. Add turmeric, ginger, paprika, coconut milk, coriander, caraway, and salt. Boil for 8 minutes, stirring constantly. Cook rice sticks in boiling water 2 minutes. Drain.

When serving, place 2 tablespoons of rice sticks in each cup and pour sauce over. Garnish with chopped egg, mint leaves, chicken, and shrimp.

CHINESE NOODLES WITH SHRIMP
Misoa Udang

6 servings

1 medium onion, minced
2 cloves garlic, minced
1 tablespoon vegetable oil
½ cup shrimp, shelled and cooked
3 cups chicken stock
  salt and pepper to taste
4 medium eggs
½ pound Chinese noodles*
½ cup chopped celery
½ cup fried crisp onion flakes (*see index*)

Brown onion and garlic in oil. Add shrimp, stock, pepper, and salt and cook 5 minutes. Break whole raw eggs in boiling sauce mixture and poach about 10 minutes, or until eggs are done. Add noodles and stir constantly for 5 minutes. Garnish with celery and onion flakes. Serve piping hot.

Variation: CHINESE NOODLES WITH ZUCCHINI

Misoa Sajur

6 servings

Follows same procedure as in Chinese Noodles with Shrimp, but add 2 cups of cubed zucchini to noodle mixture. Cook 3 minutes.

CHAPTER 7

SOUPS

VEGETABLE SOUP

Sop Sajur

6 servings

5 cups beef or chicken stock
1 cup cubed carrots
1 cup shredded white cabbage
½ cup chopped celery
½ cup chopped scallion
salt and pepper to taste
½ teaspoon ground cinnamon
½ teaspoon ground nutmeg
½ cup fried crisp onion flakes (*see index*)

Bring stock to a boil, then add carrots, cabbage, celery, scallion, salt, pepper, cinnamon, and nutmeg. Reduce heat and simmer 20 minutes. Serve hot, with onion flakes on top.

TOMATO SOUP

Sop Tomat

6 servings

5 medium tomatoes
1 medium onion, minced
1 clove garlic, minced
½ cup butter (1 stick)
5 cups beef or chicken stock
½ cup chopped scallion
½ cup chopped celery
½ teaspoon ground cinnamon
½ teaspoon ground nutmeg
salt and pepper to taste
1 teaspoon cornstarch, dissolved in 2 tablespoons
water
½ cup fried crisp onion flakes (*see index*)

Put tomatoes in boiling water and cook for 3 minutes. Remove, skin, and press through a sieve. Brown onion and garlic in butter, then add stock, chopped scallion, celery, tomatoes, and spices. Add cornstarch-water mixture to stock. Boil for 15 minutes. Serve hot, with onion flakes on top.

MUSHROOM SOUP

Sop Djamur

6 servings

5 cups chicken stock
2 cups chopped mushrooms
1 medium onion, minced
1 stalk scallion, chopped

½ teaspoon ground cinnamon
½ teaspoon ground nutmeg
1 teaspoon cornstarch,
    dissolved in 2 tablespoons water
    salt and pepper to taste
½ cup fried crisp onion flakes (*see index*)

Bring stock to a boil, then add all ingredients except cornstarch and onion flakes. Add cornstarch-water mixture to stock. Simmer 15 minutes. Serve hot, with onion flakes on top.

CURRY SOUP

Sop Kerie

6 servings

1 medium onion, minced
1 stalk scallion, minced
¼ cup butter (½ stick)
1½ tablespoons curry powder*
5 cups chicken stock
    salt and pepper to taste
1 cup chopped beef
1 teaspoon cornstarch,
    dissolved in 2 tablespoons water
½ cup chopped celery

Brown onion and scallion in butter. Add curry powder, stock, salt, and pepper and bring to a boil. Form small balls of beef. Drop them into boiling stock, reduce heat, and simmer 20 minutes. Add cornstarch-water mixture and simmer 2 minutes longer. Serve hot, with celery on top.

BIRD'S-NEST SOUP

Sop Sarang Burung

6 servings

½ cup bird's-nest*
5 cups chicken stock
½ cup shredded chicken
½ cup chopped Smithfield ham
1 stalk celery, chopped
   salt and pepper to taste
½ cup fried crisp onion flakes (*see index*)

Soak bird's-nest for 3 hours in water. Drain and add to chicken stock, together with chicken, ham, celery, salt, and pepper. Boil 15 minutes. Serve hot, with onion flakes on top.

CHICKEN LIVER SOUP

Sop Hati Ajam

6 servings

1 medium onion, minced
1 stalk celery, chopped
¼ cup butter (½ stick)
1 cup chopped chicken livers
1 tablespoon soy sauce
   salt and pepper to taste
5 cups chicken stock
1 cup sliced white cabbage
1 teaspoon cornstarch, dissolved in
   2 tablespoons water
½ cup fried crisp onion flakes (*see index*)

Brown onion and celery in butter, then add livers, soy sauce, salt, and pepper. Simmer 5 minutes. Add chicken stock, cabbage, and cornstarch-water mixture. Cook 10 minutes longer. Serve hot, with onion flakes on top.

ABALONE SOUP

Sop Pauhie

6 servings

1 can abalone (1 pound)*
5 cups chicken stock
3 slices ginger (*see index*)
½ cup sliced mushrooms
½ cup sliced Smithfield ham
1 cup sliced chicken
1 stalk celery, chopped
   salt and pepper to taste
½ cup fried crisp onion flakes (*see index*)

Drain abalone, reserving the liquid, then slice. Add abalone liquid to chicken stock and bring to a boil. Add ginger, sliced abalone, mushrooms, ham, chicken, celery, salt, and pepper. Reduce heat and simmer 30 minutes. Serve hot, with onion flakes on top.

CUCUMBER SOUP

Sop Ketimun

6 servings

2 medium cucumbers
1 medium onion, minced
1 stalk scallion, minced
¼ cup butter (½ stick)
5 cups chicken stock
1 stalk celery, minced
   salt and pepper to taste
½ cup Smithfield ham,
   cut in strips 1 inch by ½ inch
2 medium eggs, beaten
½ cup fried crisp onion flakes (*see index*)

Peel cucumbers, remove seeds, and cut into ½-inch slices. Brown onion and scallion in butter. Add stock, cucumber, celery, salt, pepper, and ham. Boil 15 minutes. Pour beaten eggs into boiling stock, reduce heat, and simmer 8 minutes longer. Serve hot, with onion flakes on top.

SHARK'S-FIN SOUP

Haaievinnen Sop

6 servings

3 sheets shark's fin *
5 cups chicken stock
1 cup shredded chicken
1 cup chopped ham
3 slices ginger

1 tablespoon cornstarch,
    dissolved in 3 tablespoons water
    salt and pepper to taste
½ cup fried crisp onion flakes (*see index*)
2 teaspoons vinegar
2 tablespoons soy sauce

Rinse and soak shark's fin in water for 6 hours, changing water every 2 hours, until fins are soft. Put fins into boiling water and cook 5 minutes. Rinse under cold water and drain. Add to chicken stock. Bring to a boil, reduce heat, and simmer 40 minutes. Add chicken, ham, ginger, cornstarch-water mixture, salt, and pepper, and simmer 10 minutes longer. Serve hot, with onion flakes on top and soy sauce and vinegar on the side.

BEAN CAKE SOUP

Sop Tahu

2 servings

3 cups chicken stock
2 bean cakes*
¼ cup chopped celery
    salt and pepper to taste
½ cup fried crisp onion flakes (*see index*)

Bring stock to a boil. Slice bean cakes and add to boiling stock. Add celery, salt, and pepper. Reduce heat and simmer 10 minutes. Serve hot, with onion flakes on top.

PORK TRIPE SOUP

Sop Tito

6 servings

> 1 whole pork tripe
> 1 cup rock salt
> 5 cups chicken stock
> 1 cup shredded chicken
> 2 stalks celery
> 5 slices ginger (*see index*)
> 1 cup shining noodles*
> 1 cup Smithfield ham,
>   cut in strips 1 inch by ½ inch
> 1 cup sliced cauliflower
> ½ cup fried crisp onion flakes (*see index*)
> 1 tablespoon crushed hot red pepper*
> 3 tablespoons lemon juice
> 2 tablespoons soy sauce

Turn tripe inside out, sprinkle with rock salt, and rub thoroughly, then scrub with a stiff brush. Repeat this procedure several times, until slippery coating is removed. Place tripe in boiling water for 5 minutes. Discard water. Cut tripe in pieces about 1 inch square. Put tripe in chicken stock and simmer 2 hours, until tripe is tender. Add chicken, celery, ginger, shining noodles, and ham. Simmer 15 minutes longer. Two minutes before serving, add cauliflower. Serve with onion flakes on top. Mix hot pepper with lemon juice and serve this and soy sauce on the side.

CHAPTER 8

SEA FOOD

FRIED SHRIMP

Udang Goreng Asam

4 servings

1 pound large shrimp, shelled or unshelled[1]
½ cup tamarind juice (*see index*) or lemon juice
salt to taste
2 cups vegetable oil

Mix shrimp with tamarind juice and salt. Boil on high heat until all liquid has been absorbed. Heat oil and fry shrimp until light brown. Drain on absorbent paper.

[1] Shrimp can be fried shelled or unshelled.

PHOENIX TAIL SHRIMP

Udang Goreng Tepung

4 servings

> 1 pound large shrimp
> 1 cup flour
> ½ cup water
>   salt to taste
> 2 teaspoons baking powder
> 2 cups vegetable oil

Wash shrimp and remove all except tail section of shell. Split shrimp halfway through down the back, clean, rinse, and dry. Prepare batter by mixing flour, water, salt and baking powder. Dip shrimp in batter and fry in deep fat until golden brown. Drain on absorbent paper.

BATTER-FRIED SHRIMP

Udang Goreng

4 servings

> 1 pound medium shrimp
> 1 medium egg
> ¼ cup flour
>   salt and pepper to taste
> 2 cups vegetable oil
> 2 lemons, cut in wedges

Shell and clean shrimp. Split by cutting halfway through. Make batter from egg, flour, salt, and pepper. Dip shrimp in batter and deep fry in hot oil until light brown. Drain on absorbent paper and serve with lemon wedges.

Variation: BATTER-FRIED FISH

Ikan Goreng Tepung

4 servings

Follow same procedure as in Batter-Fried Shrimp, but re-place shrimp with 1 pound fish fillets cut into 2-inch slices.

BUTTERFLY SHRIMP WITH HAM

Udang Gulung Ham

4 servings

1 pound large shrimp
½ cup flour
   salt and pepper to taste
1 egg, beaten
1 teaspoon baking soda
¼ cup water
½ pound Smithfield ham,
   thinly sliced (3-by-3-inch pieces)
2 cups vegetable oil

Shell and clean shrimp. Split, by cutting halfway through, and flatten out. Prepare batter by mixing flour, salt, pepper, egg, baking soda, and water. Place a piece of ham around each shrimp, dip in batter, and deep fry until golden brown. Drain on absorbent paper.

Variation 1: BUTTERFLY SHRIMP WITH BACON

Udang Gulung Spek

4 servings

Follow the same procedure as in Butterfly Shrimp with Ham, but replace ham with ½ pound of bacon strips.

Variation 2: FRIED FISH WITH HAM

Ikan Gulung Ham

4 servings

Follow same procedure as in Butterfly Shrimp with Ham, but replace shrimp with 1 pound of fish fillets, cut in 2-inch slices.

Variation 3: FRIED FISH WITH BACON

Ikan Gulung Spek

4 servings

Follow same procedure as in Butterfly Shrimp with Ham, but replace shrimp with 1 pound of fish fillets, cut in 2-inch slices, and ham with ½ pound of bacon strips.

SAUTÉED SHRIMP WITH GINGER

Udang Tumis Djahe

4 servings

1 pound shrimp
1 tablespoon vegetable oil
2 tablespoons soy sauce
1 tablespoon sugar
1 tablespoon vinegar
1 tablespoon chopped ginger°
  salt and pepper to taste
2 tablespoons sherry

Shell and clean shrimp. Rinse and dry. In a skillet, heat together oil, soy sauce, sugar, vinegar, salt, pepper, and ginger. Add shrimp and cook over high heat 5 minutes. One minute before serving, add sherry. Serve hot.

BOILED SHRIMP

Udang Rebus

4 servings

1 pound medium shrimp
1 cup water
  salt to taste
1 teaspoon French mustard
1 teaspoon chopped ginger*
1 tablespoon sugar
1 tablespoon vinegar
1 tablespoon soy sauce

Rinse shrimp, put into 1 cup of boiling water. Add salt. Cook for 8 minutes, drain, and shell. Serve with sauce made by mixing mustard, ginger, sugar, vinegar, and soy sauce.

SHRIMP WITH GREEN PEPPER

Udang Masak Tjabe Hidjau

4 servings

1 pound medium shrimp
1 tablespoon cornstarch
2 large green peppers
2 tablespoons vegetable oil
2 tablespoons sherry
salt and pepper to taste

Shell shrimp, split in half. Mix with cornstarch. Quarter green peppers, remove seeds, and cut each quarter in 3 pieces. Sauté shrimp in oil for 5 minutes. Add sherry, stir 1 minute, and remove shrimp. Cook peppers in the liquid for 2 minutes over high heat. Add shrimp, salt, and pepper, and stir for 3 minutes. Serve hot.

SHRIMP WITH CUCUMBER

Tumis Udang Pakai Ketimun

4 servings

1 pound medium shrimp
1 tablespoon cornstarch
salt and pepper to taste
2 medium cucumbers
1 medium onion, minced
2 tablespoons vegetable oil
¼ cup fried crisp onion flakes (*see index*)

Shell shrimp, then split and clean. Drain. Mix with cornstarch, salt, and pepper. Peel and split cucumbers in half lengthwise, then cut crosswise into ¼-inch sections. Remove seeds. Fry onion in oil, add shrimp, and stir 5 minutes. Add cucumbers and cook 5 minutes longer. Serve hot, with onion flakes on top.

FRIED SHRIMP BALLS
Bakso Udang Goreng

4 servings

1 pound medium shrimp
  salt and pepper to taste
1 egg white, beaten stiff
2 cups vegetable oil
1 lemon, cut in wedges

Shell shrimp, then clean and chop it into a fine paste. Add salt, pepper, and egg white. Make balls from mixture, drop into hot oil, and fry until golden brown. Serve with lemon wedges.

SHRIMP WITH ALMONDS
Udang Masak Amandel

4 servings

1 pound medium shrimp
2 stalks celery
½ cup blanched almonds
2 tablespoons vegetable oil
1 medium onion, minced
2 tablespoons sherry
  salt and pepper to taste
½ cup crisp onion flakes (*see index*)

Shell shrimp, then clean, dry, and dice. Dice celery. Chop almonds coarsely. Heat oil and fry onion for 2 minutes. Add shrimp, sherry, almonds, celery, salt and pepper. Stir 5 minutes over high heat. Serve hot, with onion flakes on top.

CURRIED SHRIMP

Udang Kerie

4 servings

1 pound medium shrimp
1 tablespoon vegetable oil
1 medium onion, minced
2 cloves garlic, minced
1 tablespoon curry powder*
1 cup milk or coconut milk*
¼ cup shining noodles*
1 bay leaf
1 teaspoon ground coriander
1 teaspoon ground caraway

Shell shrimp, then clean and drain. Heat oil and fry onion and garlic for 2 minutes. Add shrimp, curry powder, coconut milk, shining noodles, bay leaf, coriander, and caraway. Bring to a boil, reduce heat, and simmer 15 minutes.

Variation: CURRIED FISH

Ikan Masak Kerie

4 servings

Follow same procedure as in Curried Shrimp, but replace shrimp with 1 pound of fish fillets, cut in 2-inch slices.

SAUTÉED SHRIMP WITH VEGETABLES
Udang Tjha

4 servings

1 pound medium shrimp
2 medium onions, minced
2 cloves garlic, minced
½ cup Smithfield ham,
   sliced in strips 1 inch long by ⅛ inch wide
2 tablespoons soy sauce
   salt and pepper to taste
1 cup white cabbage, cut in 1½-inch squares
½ cup sliced bamboo shoots*
2 stalks celery, diced
½ cup fried crisp onion flakes (*see index*)

Shell shrimp and split, cutting halfway through. Wash and drain. Brown onions and garlic in oil for 2 minutes. Add shrimp, ham, soy sauce, salt, pepper, cabbage, and bamboo shoots. Cook 10 minutes. One minute before serving, add celery. Serve hot, with onion flakes on top.

Variation: SAUTÉED FISH WITH VEGETABLES

Ikan Tjha

4 servings

Follow same procedure as in Sautéed Shrimp with Vegetables, but replace shrimp with 1 pound of fish fillets, cut in 2-inch slices.

SHRIMP WITH SNOW PEAS

Udang Masak Katjang Kapri

4 servings

1 pound medium shrimp
1 medium onion, minced
2 tablespoons vegetable oil
2 tablespoons soy sauce
    salt and pepper to taste
1 tablespoon sherry
1 cup whole snow peas *
½ cup fried crisp onion flakes (*see index*)

Shell shrimp and split, cutting halfway through. Clean and dry. Fry onion in oil for 2 minutes. Add shrimp, soy sauce, salt, pepper, and sherry. Cook for 10 minutes. One minute before serving, add snow peas and stir. Serve hot, with onion flakes on top.

Variation: FISH WITH SNOW PEAS

Ikan Masak Katjang Kapri

4 servings

Follow same procedure as in Shrimp with Snow Peas, but replace shrimp with 1 pound of fish fillets, cut in 2-inch slices.

SHRIMP WITH TOMATO SAUCE

Udang Masak Saos Tomat

4 servings

1 pound medium shrimp
1 clove garlic, minced
1 tablespoon vegetable oil
 salt and pepper to taste
¼ cup water
1 tablespoon sugar
4 tablespoons ketchup
1 teaspoon cornstarch,
 dissolved in 2 tablespoons water

Shell shrimp, then clean and dry. Split, cutting halfway through. Boil 3 minutes over high heat. Brown garlic in oil, add salt, pepper, water, sugar, ketchup, and shrimp. Bring to a boil. Add cornstarch-water mixture and stir 5 minutes more. Serve hot.

Variation: FISH WITH TOMATO SAUCE

Ikan Masak Saos Tomat

4 servings

Follow same procedure as in Shrimp with Tomato Sauce, but replace shrimp with 1 pound of fish fillets, cut in 2-inch slices.

SHRIMP WITH OYSTER SAUCE

Udang Masak Saos Tiram

4 servings

1 pound large shrimp
1 tablespoon soy sauce
½ cup oyster sauce*
1 tablespoon cornstarch,
dissolved in 2 tablespoons water

Remove head and legs of shrimp, and slit shell to clean, but leave shell on.[1] Heat frying pan, add shrimp, and panbroil for 2 minutes. Add soy sauce, oyster sauce, and cornstarch-water mixture. Stir constantly, over high heat, until moisture has been absorbed. Serve hot or cold.

SHRIMP WITH BEAN SPROUTS

Udang Masak Tauge

4 servings

1 pound shrimp
1 tablespoon vegetable oil
1 clove garlic, minced
1 slice ginger
salt and pepper to taste
1 cup bean sprouts*

Shell shrimp. Split, cutting halfway through. Heat oil. Add garlic and ginger and fry 1 minute. Add shrimp and cook 5 minutes. Add salt, pepper, and bean sprouts. Stir 2 minutes and serve hot.

[1] The fun here is to remove the shell with the tongue.

Variation 1: SHRIMP WITH CHINESE CABBAGE

Udang Masak Sajur Petsay

4 servings

Follow same procedure as in Shrimp with Bean Sprouts, but replace the bean sprouts with 1 cup shredded Chinese cabbage.* Cook the cabbage 5 minutes.

Variation 2: SHRIMP

WITH CHINESE VEGETABLES

Udang Tjha Sajur

4 servings

Follow same procedure as in Shrimp with Bean Sprouts, but add ½ cup of snow peas,* ½ cup sliced Chinese mushrooms,* and ½ cup diced water chestnuts.* Soak dried mushrooms 2 hours, drain, and slice. Cook all vegetables 5 minutes before serving.

SHRIMP WITH SOY SAUCE

Udang Pindang Ketjap

4 servings

> 1 pound medium shrimp
> 2 tablespoons soy sauce
> 1 medium onion, minced
> 2 bay leaves
> 1 hot red pepper, split in half*
> ¼ cup tamarind juice (see index) or lemon juice
> salt to taste
> 1 cup water

Shell shrimp, then clean and split, cutting halfway through. Rinse and dry. Put all the ingredients in a skillet. Bring to a boil, reduce heat, and simmer 20 minutes. Serve.

Variation: FISH WITH SOY SAUCE

Ikan Pindang Ketjap

4 servings

Follow same procedure as in Shrimp with Soy Sauce, but substitute 2 pounds of fish (porgy, carp, pike, or sea bass) for the shrimp. Fish should be cleaned, cut in 3-inch slices, and wiped dry.

SHRIMP IN RED PEPPER SAUCE
Udang Masak Goreng Asam

4 servings

1 pound large shrimp
1 teaspoon shrimp paste*
1 tablespoon vegetable oil
2 tablespoons ground hot red pepper*
1 tablespoon paprika
½ cup tamarind juice (*see index*) or lemon juice
salt to taste

Shell and clean shrimp. Heat oil and brown onion and shrimp paste. Add red pepper, paprika, tamarind juice, salt, and shrimp. Bring to a boil, reduce heat, and simmer 20 minutes.

Variation: FISH IN RED PEPPER SAUCE

Ikan Masak Goreng Asam

6 servings

Follow same procedure as in Shrimp in Red Pepper Sauce, but substitute 2 pounds fish (porgy, carp, pike, or sea bass) for the shrimp and add 2 cups of water. Fish should be cleaned, cut in 3-inch slices, and wiped dry.

SHRIMP BALLS WITH BROTH

Bakso Udang

4 servings

1 pound medium shrimp
salt and pepper to taste
1 medium egg
5 cups chicken stock
1 cup shredded white cabbage
½ cup shining noodles*
¼ cup chopped celery
¼ cup fried crisp onion flakes (see index)

Shell shrimp, then clean, rinse, dry, and chop. Add salt, pepper, and egg to shrimp paste, mix, and make into balls. Bring stock to a boil, add shrimp balls, and cook 5 minutes. Add cabbage and shining noodles. Simmer 10 minutes. Serve hot, with celery and onion flakes on top.

Variation: FISH BALLS WITH BROTH

Bakso Ikan

4 servings

Follow same procedure as in Shrimp Balls with Broth, but replace shrimp with 1 pound of chopped fish fillets.

CHICKEN STUFFED WITH SHRIMP

Udang Gulung Ajam

4 servings

1 pound medium shrimp
salt and pepper to taste
2 chicken breasts
2 tablespoons cornstarch
2 tablespoons vegetable oil
1 medium onion, minced
1 tablespoon soy sauce
½ cup chicken broth
1 cup cooked peas
½ cup fried crisp onion flakes (*see index*)

Shell shrimp, then clean, rinse, dry, and chop. Add salt and pepper and mix. Cut chicken in thin slices. Put 1 teaspoon shrimp paste on each slice and roll up. Close both ends with a little cornstarch. Heat oil and fry chicken rolls on high heat for 5 minutes. Add onion and stir 1 minute. Add soy sauce and broth and simmer 10 minutes. One minute before serving, add peas. Garnish with onion flakes.

MUSHROOMS STUFFED WITH PORK AND SHRIMP

Djamur Isi Udang

4 servings

10 large Chinese mushrooms *
½ pound medium shrimp
½ cup chopped pork
1 stalk celery, chopped
salt and pepper to taste
2 tablespoons vegetable oil
2 tablespoons soy sauce
½ cup water

Soak mushrooms in water for 1 hour, drain, and remove stems. Shell shrimp, then clean and chop. Mix shrimp with pork, celery, salt, and pepper. Fill mushroom cavities with this mixture. Heat oil. Place mushrooms in hot oil, add soy sauce and water, and bring to a boil. Simmer 10 minutes on low heat. Serve hot.

SHRIMP WITH CHINESE MUSHROOMS
Udang Masak Djamur Kering

4 servings

1 pound medium shrimp
4 large Chinese mushrooms*
1 tablespoon vegetable oil
1 medium onion, minced
  salt and pepper to taste
1 tablespoon sherry

Shell shrimp, then clean and dry. Soak mushrooms in water for 2 hours. Drain and cut in slices. Heat oil and fry onion for 2 minutes. Add shrimp, salt, pepper, mushrooms, and sherry and simmer 10 minutes. Serve hot.

Variation: FISH WITH CHINESE MUSHROOMS
Ikan Masak Djamur Kering

4 servings

Follow same procedure as in Shrimp with Chinese Mushrooms, but replace shrimp with 1 pound fish fillets, cut in 2-inch slices.

SWEET-AND-SOUR SHRIMP
Udang Asam Manis

4 servings

1 medium egg
4 tablespoons flour
  salt to taste

1 cup water
1 pound large shrimp
2 cups vegetable oil
4 slices ginger (*see index*)
½ cup vinegar
¼ cup shredded green peppers
¼ cup sliced carrots
¼ cup pineapple, sliced and cut in wedges
4 tablespoons sugar
1 tablespoon soy sauce
2 teaspoons cornstarch,
  dissolved in 4 tablespoons water

Mix a batter of egg, flour, salt and ½ cup of the water. Shell shrimp, then clean and split, cutting halfway through. Rinse and dry. Dip shrimp in batter and deep fry in hot oil (370°) for 3 minutes. Remove and place in a serving dish. Remove most of the oil, leaving 2 tablespoons in skillet. Heat this and add ginger, the rest of the water, vinegar, green peppers, carrots, pineapple, sugar, soy sauce, and salt. Bring to a boil and stir for 5 minutes. Stir in cornstarch-water mixture and boil for 2 minutes. Pour mixture over shrimp and serve immediately.

Variation: SWEET-AND-SOUR FISH

Ang Sio Hie

6 *servings*

Follow same procedure as in Sweet-and-Sour Shrimp, but substitute 2 pounds fish (porgy, carp, pike, or sea bass) for the shrimp.

Clean fish and wipe dry. Make 2 diagonal slashes on each side of the fish and rub fish with salt. After heating oil to 375°, fry fish, 5 minutes on each side. Turn only once. Drain off oil. Pour sweet-and-sour mixture over fish and serve immediately.

FRIED FISH

Ikan Goreng

6 servings

2 pounds fish (porgy, carp, pike, or sea bass)
   salt to taste
2 cups vegetable oil

Clean fish and wipe dry. Make 2 diagonal slashes on each side of fish and rub fish with salt. Heat oil to 375° and fry fish, 5 minutes on each side. Turn only once. Drain off oil.

Variation: **FRIED FISH WITH TAMARIND JUICE**

Ikan Goreng Asam

6 servings

2 pounds fish (porgy, carp, pike, or sea bass)
¼ cup tamarind juice (*see index*) or lemon juice
   salt to taste
2 cups vegetable oil

Rub fish with a mixture of tamarind juice and salt and let stand 20 minutes before frying. Then follow same procedure as in Fried Fish.

FRIED FISH WITH RED PEPPER

Ikan Goreng Belada

6 servings

2 pounds fish (porgy, carp, pike, or sea bass),
fried *see p. 78*)
2 tablespoons vegetable oil
½ cup ground hot red peppers*
1 medium onion, minced
salt to taste
2 tablespoons lemon juice

Heat oil. Add red peppers, onion, and salt and fry 2 minutes. Add lemon juice and stir 2 minutes longer. Pour mixture over fried fish.

FRIED FISH WITH SOYBEAN SAUCE

Ikan Goreng Taotjo, Ikan Tjin Tjoan

6 servings

2 pounds fish (porgy, carp, pike, or sea bass),
fried *see p. 78*)
2 tablespoons oil
1 medium onion, minced
1 tablespoon ginger, cut julienne
2 tablespoons salted soybeans*
1 tablespoon vinegar
½ cup water
1 teaspoon cornstarch,
dissolved in 2 tablespoons water

Heat oil. Add onion and ginger and fry 2 minutes. Add soybeans, vinegar, cornstarch-water mixture, and water, and stir and boil for 5 minutes. Pour mixture over fried fish and serve immediately.

FISH WITH COCONUT MILK

Ikan Masak Kelapa

6 servings

2 pounds fish (porgy, carp, pike, or sea bass)
2 cups coconut milk*
1 tablespoon ground hot red pepper*
½ teaspoon turmeric*
   salt to taste
10 mint leaves

Clean fish and cut into 3-inch slices. Put in a pan, add coconut milk, red pepper, turmeric, salt, and mint leaves. Bring to a boil, reduce heat, and simmer 20 minutes.

FISH IN RED PEPPER SAUCE

Ikan Pangeh

6 servings

2 pounds fish (porgy, carp, pike, or sea bass)
½ cup tamarind juice (see index)
½ cup ground hot red peppers*
½ cup water
10 mint leaves
   salt to taste

Clean fish and make 2 diagonal slices on each side of fish. Put in a pan, add tamarind juice, red pepper, water, mint leaves, and salt. Bring to a boil, reduce heat, and simmer 20 minutes.

FISH WITH FRESH MUSHROOMS

Ikan Masak Djamur

4 servings

1 pound fish fillets, cut in 1-inch slices
1 tablespoon vegetable oil
1 medium onion, minced
1 pound mushrooms, sliced
1 tablespoon soy sauce
 salt and pepper to taste
1 tablespoon sherry
1 stalk celery, chopped

Wash and dry fish. Heat oil and fry onion for 2 minutes. Add mushrooms, soy sauce, salt, pepper, sherry, and fish. Stir gently and cook for 10 minutes. Serve hot, with celery on top.

MARINATED FISH

Ikan Tjuka

6 servings

2 pounds fish (porgy, carp, pike, or sea bass)
1 tablespoon oil
4 cloves garlic
1 medium onion, sliced
5 slices ginger
2 cups vinegar
1 teaspoon turmeric*
 salt to taste

Clean fish, cut in 3-inch slices, and drain. Heat oil and fry whole garlic cloves, onion, and ginger 2 minutes. Add vinegar, turmeric, salt, and fish. Bring to a boil, reduce heat, and simmer for 20 minutes.

This fish will taste better when kept several days in vinegar mixture. Serve cold.

Variation: MARINATED FRIED FISH

Ikan Goreng Tjuka

6 servings

Follow same procedure as in Marinated Fish, but deep fry fish, (*see index for* Fried Fish) before putting it into vinegar mixture.

BAKED SALTED FISH

Ikan Asin Bakar

6 servings

1 pound dried fish, salted*

Any kind of salted fish can be used. Wash fish, cut in 2-inch slices, and wrap in aluminum foil. Put into 325° oven for 30 minutes, or until fish is done. Serve plain, with rice.

SALTED FISH WITH TOMATOES

Ikan Asin Tomat

6 servings

1 pound dried fish, salted*
2 cups vegetable oil
2 medium onions, sliced
½ cup sliced hot red peppers*
¼ cup lemon juice
3 medium tomatoes, cut in wedges

Wash fish and cut in 1-inch slices. Heat oil and fry fish until light brown. Drain. Brown onion and red pepper in 2 tablespoons of the oil. Add lemon juice and tomatoes and simmer 1 minute. Pour mixture over fish.

BARBECUED FISH WITH COCONUT MILK

Ikan Sambam

6 servings

1 whole fish, about 2 pounds
    (porgy, carp, pike, or sea bass)
2 cups coconut milk*
1 tablespoon ground hot red pepper*
1 teaspoon turmeric*
    salt to taste
10 mint leaves (*optional*)

Wash fish and cut diagonal slashes on each side, and put in oven-proof dish. Mix coconut milk with red pepper, turmeric, salt, and mint leaves. Pour this mixture over fish, put in moderate oven (350°), and bake for 30 minutes, or until fish is done.

Variation: BARBECUED FISH WITH SOY SAUCE

Ikan Sambam Ketjap

6 servings

1 whole 2-pound fish
    (porgy, carp, pike, or sea bass)
½ cup melted butter
2 tablespoons soy sauce
2 tablespoons lemon juice
1 tablespoon ground hot red pepper*
    salt and pepper to taste

Follow same procedure as in Barbecued Fish with Coconut Milk, but use as sauce a mixture of melted butter, soy sauce, lemon juice, red pepper, salt, and pepper.

STEAMED FISH

Ikan Tim

6 servings

1 whole 2-pound fish
(porgy, carp, pike, or sea bass)
2 tablespoons sherry
2 tablespoons soy sauce
2 tablespoons shredded ginger*
½ cup melted butter
2 tablespoons chopped scallion
salt and pepper to taste

Clean fish, then wash, drain, and place in heat-proof dish. Mix sherry, soy sauce, ginger, butter, scallion, salt, and pepper. Pour this mixture over fish and steam 1 hour, or until fish is done.

STEAMED FISH WITH HAM
AND CHINESE MUSHROOMS

Ikan Tim Pakai Ham Dan Djamur

6 servings

1 whole 2-pound fish
(porgy, carp, pike, or sea bass)
3 large Chinese mushrooms*
¼ cup Smithfield ham, cut julienne
2 tablespoons chopped ginger*
1 tablespoon soy sauce
salt and pepper to taste
½ cup melted butter
1 tablespoon chopped scallion

Clean fish, then wash, drain, and place in heat-proof dish. Soak mushrooms for ½ hour in water, drain, and slice. Mix with all other ingredients and pour over fish. Cover and steam 1 hour, or until fish is done.

Variation: *STEAMED FISH WITH BEAN CAKE*

Ikan Tim Pakai Tahu

6 *servings*

Follow same procedure as in Steamed Fish but replace ham with 3 bean cakes, cubed.*

SHAD ROE

Telur Trubuk

2 *servings*

½ pound shad roe
2 tablespoons flour
2 cups vegetable oil
1 medium onion, minced
½ cup sliced hot red pepper*
1 tablespoon lemon juice
  salt to taste

Clean and dry roe, then cover with flour. Heat oil (350°) in a skillet and deep fry roe until golden brown. Remove roe, drain. Leave 1 tablespoon oil in skillet and fry onion and red pepper for 2 minutes. Add lemon juice and salt and stir 1 minute. Add roe, stir 1 minute longer, and serve.

SAUTÉED SQUID WITH TOMATOES

Tjumi-Tjumi Tjha

2 servings

4 large squid
1 tablespoon vegetable oil
1 medium onion, minced
2 cloves garlic, minced
1 tablespoon sherry
   salt and pepper to taste
2 medium tomatoes, cut in wedges
½ cup water

Wash squid, cut down lengthwise, and remove jelly-like material and tentacles. Slash squid slightly on one side, making diamond patterns. Cut each in 4 pieces and drain. Heat oil and add squid. On high heat, fry until squid begins to curl. Add onion, garlic, sherry, salt, pepper, tomatoes, and water, and simmer 10 minutes. Serve hot.

SAUTÉED ABALONE

Pauhie Tjha

6 servings

1 1-pound can of abalone*
1 medium onion
2 cloves garlic, minced
2 tablespoons vegetable oil
½ cup Smithfield ham, cut in strips
   2 inches long by ½ inch wide
½ cup shrimp, shelled and cooked

1 tablespoon soy sauce
1 cup sliced bamboo shoots*
1 cup shredded cabbage
  salt and pepper to taste
½ cup chicken stock
3 stalks celery, cut julienne

Slice abalone. Fry onion and garlic in hot oil for 2 minutes. Add sliced abalone, ham, shrimp, soy sauce, bamboo shoots, cabbage, salt, pepper, and stock. Simmer 10 minutes. One minute before serving, add celery. Serve hot.

BRAISED ABALONE IN OYSTER SAUCE

Tjha Pauhie Saos Tiram

6 servings

1 1-pound can abalone*
1 medium onion, minced
1 tablespoon vegetable oil
1 cup Smithfield ham,
  cut in strips 2 inches long by ⅛ inch wide
¼ cup oyster sauce*
1 tablespoon soy sauce
  salt and pepper to taste
1 sprig parsley, chopped

Slice abalone, reserving ½ cup of the liquid. Fry onion in hot oil for 2 minutes. Add sliced abalone, ham, oyster sauce, soy sauce, salt, pepper, and abalone liquid. Simmer 10 minutes. Serve hot, with chopped parsley on top.

CHAPTER 9

MEATS

PORK BALLS WITH BROTH
Bakso Babi

4 servings

1 pound lean pork, chopped
   salt and pepper to taste
¼ cup chopped celery
1 tablespoon chopped onion
1 teaspoon chopped garlic
4 cups water
½ cup shining noodles*
2 cups shredded white cabbage
½ cup fried crisp onion flakes (*see index*)

Mix pork with salt, pepper, celery, onion, and garlic. Form into balls with a teaspoon and drop into boiling water. Simmer on low heat 20 minutes. Add shining noodles and cabbage and cook 5 minutes longer. Serve hot, with onion flakes on top.

PORK BALLS WITH SHRIMP
Bakso Pong

4 servings

½ cup chopped pork
½ cup shrimp, chopped and cooked
1 bean cake, chopped*
¼ cup chopped bamboo shoots*
   salt and pepper to taste
¼ cup chopped celery
1 tablespoon chopped onion
2 medium eggs
2 cups vegetable oil
2 cloves garlic, minced
4 cups chicken stock
1 cup shredded white cabbage
2 tablespoons soy sauce
½ cup shining noodles*
½ cup snow peas*
½ cup fried crisp onion flakes (see index)

Mix pork with shrimp, bean cake, bamboo shoots, salt, pepper, celery, onion, and eggs. Form into balls with a teaspoon and drop into hot oil (350°). Fry until light brown and drain. Remove oil, leaving 1 tablespoon in skillet. Heat and fry garlic for 1 minute. Add stock, cabbage, soy sauce, meat balls, and shining noodles. Bring to a boil and simmer 5 minutes. One minute before serving, add snow peas. Serve hot, with onion flakes on top.

STUFFED BEAN CAKE
Bakso Tahu

4 servings

4 Chinese bean cakes*
1 cup chopped pork
1 tablespoon chopped shrimp
2 tablespoons cornstarch
1 tablespoon chopped celery
    salt and pepper to taste
2 cups vegetable oil

Cut bean cakes diagonally in half. With a teaspoon, make a cavity in each bean cake's diagonal side. The cavity should be as large as possible. Mix pork, shrimp, cornstarch, celery, salt, and pepper and fill cavity in bean cake with this mixture. Deep fry in hot oil (375°) until light brown. Drain. Serve with Peanut Sauce (*see index*).

PORK WITH SOY SAUCE
Babi Ketjap

4 servings

1 pound lean pork
    salt to taste
2 tablespoons soy sauce
½ cup water

Cut pork in 1-inch cubes. Put in skillet, add salt, soy sauce and water. Bring to a boil, reduce heat, and simmer 20 minutes, or until meat is tender and thoroughly cooked.

PORK WITH SOY SAUCE AND POTATOES
Babi Tjin

4 servings

1 pound lean pork
½ cup vegetable oil
½ pound potatoes
1 medium onion, minced
3 cloves garlic, minced
2 tablespoons soy sauce
　salt and pepper to taste
2 tablespoons ground dried shrimp*
1 tablespoon brown sugar
½ cup water

Cut pork in 1-inch cubes and brown in hot oil. Remove and drain. Peel potatoes, cut in 1-inch cubes, and fry until half done. Drain. Fry onion and garlic in rest of oil for 2 minutes. Add soy sauce, salt, pepper, potatoes, shrimp, sugar, pork, and water. Bring to a boil, reduce heat, and simmer 20 minutes. Serve hot.

PORK ROLL
Kee Kian

4 servings

1 pound lean pork
1 medium egg
2 tablespoons flour
　salt and pepper to taste
½ cup cubed pork fat
1 cup vegetable oil

Chop pork and mix with egg, flour, salt, pepper, and pork fat. Form into a roll and steam for 30 minutes. Cool. Heat oil in a skillet and fry pork roll until golden brown. Cut in 1-inch-thick slices, and serve with a hot sauce.*

PORK WITH MIXED VEGETABLES

Tjaptjay Goreng

6 servings

   1 chicken breast, sliced
   1 cup sliced chicken livers and gizzards
   ½ cup chicken stock
   1 medium onion, minced
   3 cloves garlic, minced
   1 tablespoon oil
   ½ cup shredded white cabbage
   1 tablespoon soy sauce
   1 cup pork balls (see index)
   1 cup sliced pork roll (see index)
   1 cup shrimp balls
     (see index for Shrimp Balls with Broth)
   1 cup snow peas*
     salt and pepper to taste
   ½ cup fried crisp onion flakes (see index)

Put chicken breast, livers and gizzards into boiling stock. Reduce heat and simmer 40 minutes. Brown onion and garlic in oil. Add to stock, along with cabbage, soy sauce, pork balls, pork roll, and shrimp balls. Bring to a boil, reduce heat, and simmer 5 minutes. One minute before serving, add snow peas, salt, and pepper. Serve, with onion flakes on top.

PORK WITH MIXED VEGETABLES AND BROTH

Tjaptjay Kua

6 servings

Follow same procedure as above, but add 3 cups of chicken stock.

BARBECUED PORK

Babi Panggang

4 servings

3 cloves garlic, chopped
1 medium onion, chopped
  salt and pepper to taste
1 tablespoon soy sauce
1 teaspoon sugar
1 tablespoon ground cinnamon
1 pound pork with skin
1 teaspoon honey
1 tablespoon sherry
¼ cup water

Mix garlic with onion, salt, pepper, soy sauce, sugar, and cinnamon. Make slashes on meat side of pork and rub in soy-sauce mixture. Place pork, skin side down, in roasting pan with about ½ inch of water in it. Roast 40 minutes in 350° oven. Turn skin side up and prick skin thoroughly. Mix honey, sherry, and water and rub into skin. Roast 2 hours longer, or until skin is brown and crisp. Cut pork in 1-inch-square pieces. Serve with mustard and hot sauce.*

PORK WITH SALTED MUSTARD GREENS

Babi Masak Sajur Asin

4 servings

1 pound lean pork
1 8-ounce can salted mustard greens
2 slices ginger (*see index*)
3 cups water
   salt to taste

Slice meat into 1-inch pieces. Put into a pan and add mustard greens, ginger, water, and salt. Bring to a boil, reduce heat, and simmer 20 minutes.

SPARERIBS WITH
SALTED MUSTARD GREENS

Tulang Babi Masak Sajur Asin

4 servings

2 pounds pork spareribs
1 8-ounce can salted mustard greens
5 cups water
2 slices ginger (*see index*)
   salt to taste

Slice spareribs through between bones, and then chop each sparerib into 3-inch pieces. Put into a pan and add mustard greens, water, ginger, and salt. Bring to a boil, reduce heat, and simmer 40 minutes, or until meat is tender.

PORK HAMBURGER

Perkedel Babi

4 servings

1½ pounds ground pork
   salt and pepper to taste
1 teaspoon ground cinnamon
1 large egg
½ stick butter (¼ cup)
1 medium onion, sliced
1 cup water
½ cup fried crisp onion flakes (*see index*)

Mix pork with salt, pepper, cinnamon, and egg. Form 4 patties of the mixture and brown in butter. Add onion and stir 2 minutes. Add water and simmer 20 minutes. Serve, with onion flakes on top.

SAUTÉED PORK CHOPS

Karbonatjie

6 servings

6 pork chops
   salt and pepper to taste
1 tablespoon ground cinnamon
2 tablespoons bread crumbs
1 stick butter (½ cup)
1 cup water

Wash pork chops, then dry and rub with salt, pepper, and cinnamon. Dip chops in bread crumbs and brown in butter. Add water, bring to a boil. Reduce heat, and simmer 30 minutes.

PORK STEAK
Bifstik Babi

4 servings

1½ pounds lean pork
  salt and pepper to taste
1 tablespoon ground cinnamon
1 teaspoon ground nutmeg
1 stick butter (½ cup)
1 cup water
1 teaspoon cornstarch,
  dissolved in 2 tablespoons water
½ cup fried crisp onion flakes (*see index*)

Wash pork, dry, and prick holes in the meat with a fork. Rub with salt, pepper, cinnamon and nutmeg. Let stand 1 hour. Brown in butter. Add water, bring to a boil, reduce heat, and simmer 30 minutes. Add cornstarch-water mixture and stir 2 minutes longer. Cut in thin slices and serve, with onion flakes on top.

PORK SAUTÉED WITH DRIED SQUID
Djuhie Tjha

4 servings

1 cup dried squid, cut julienne*
1 pound lean pork, cut julienne
1 medium onion, sliced
2 cloves garlic, sliced
¼ cup vegetable oil
2 tablespoons soy sauce
  salt and pepper to taste
½ cup shrimp, shelled and cooked
2 stalks celery, cut julienne

Wash squid twice, add ½ cup water, and soak overnight. Drain, reserving water. Brown onion and garlic in oil. Add pork, squid, soy sauce, salt, pepper, and squid water. Bring to a boil, reduce heat, and simmer 30 minutes. Add shrimp and stir 2 minutes longer. Add celery and serve immediately.

PORK WITH DRIED SALTED CABBAGE
Babi Masak Tongtjay

4 servings

1 pound lean pork, cut in pieces 1 inch long
  by ¼ inch wide
2 cups water
½ cup dried salted cabbage*

Put pork into a pan with water and cabbage and bring to a boil. Reduce heat and simmer 20 minutes. Serve hot.

PORK WITH SALTED FISH AND WHITE RADISH

Babi Masak Lobak

4 servings

1 pound lean pork, cut in pieces 1 inch long
by ¼ inch wide
¼ pound salted dried fish, cut in 1-inch slices*
3 cups water
2 slices ginger (*see index*)
1 cup white radish, cut in 1-inch cubes
2 tablespoons soy sauce

Put pork into a pan with fish, water, and ginger and bring to a boil. Reduce heat and simmer 20 minutes. Add white radish and simmer 5 minutes longer. Serve hot, with soy sauce on the side.

SAUTÉED PORK WITH BAMBOO SHOOTS

Babi Masak Rebung

4 servings

1 tablespoon vegetable oil
1 medium onion, sliced
3 cloves garlic, sliced
1 pound lean pork, cut in pieces 1 inch long
by 1 inch wide
1 cup sliced bamboo shoots*
2 tablespoons soy sauce
1 teaspoon cornstarch, dissolved in
2 tablespoons water
¼ cup fried crisp onion flakes (*see index*)

Heat oil, add onion and garlic, and fry 2 minutes. Add pork, bamboo shoots, and soy sauce. Stir and simmer 20 minutes. Two minutes before serving, add cornstarch-water mixture and stir. Serve hot, with onion flakes on top.

BRAISED PORK
Babi Tjha

4 servings

1 pound lean pork,
  cut in pieces 1 inch long by ¼ inch wide
½ cup water
2 tablespoons soy sauce
1 tablespoon sherry
1 tablespoon brown sugar
2 stalks scallion, chopped
2 cloves garlic, chopped
  salt and pepper to taste

Put pork in a pan and add water and all other ingredients. Bring to a boil, reduce heat, and simmer 20 minutes, or until meat is tender. Serve hot.

FRIED PORK BALLS
Bakso Goreng

4 servings

1 pound chopped pork
1 medium onion, chopped
1 stalk celery, chopped
2 cloves garlic, chopped
½ cup chopped mushrooms
1 medium egg
  salt and pepper to taste
1 cup vegetable oil

Mix pork with onion, celery, garlic, mushrooms, egg, salt, and pepper. Form into balls 1 inch in diameter. Fry in hot fat (375°) until golden brown.

HAM STEWED WITH CHESTNUTS
Ham Masak Kastanje

4 servings

1 pound chestnuts
1 pound Smithfield ham
2 tablespoons soy sauce
2 cups water
1 tablespoon sherry
1 tablespoon brown sugar
2 cloves garlic
1 stalk scallion, chopped
3 slices ginger (*see index*)
   salt and pepper to taste

Wash chestnuts, make a cut in each, and cook in boiling water 15 minutes. Drain and peel while hot. Cut ham into 1-inch cubes. Put in pan with soy sauce, water, sherry, sugar, garlic, scallion, ginger, salt, and pepper. Bring to a boil, reduce heat, and simmer 2 hours. Add chestnuts during the last hour of cooking. Serve hot.

SPARERIBS WITH DRIED SALTED CABBAGE
Tulang Babi Masak Tongtjay

4 servings

2 pounds pork spareribs
½ cup dried salted cabbage*
4 cups water

Slice spareribs through between bones, and then chop each sparerib into 3-inch pieces. Put spareribs into a pan and add cabbage and water. Bring to a boil, reduce heat, and simmer 1 hour, or until meat is soft.

PORK WITH SALTED WHITE RADISH

Babi Masak Lobak Asin

4 servings

1 pound lean pork,
   cut in pieces 1 inch long by 1 inch wide
4 cups water
1 cup sliced salted white radish*
2 slices ginger (see index)

Put pork into a pan with water, white radish, and ginger.
Bring to a boil, reduce heat, and simmer 20 minutes, or until
meat is tender and well done. Serve hot.

STUFFED EGGPLANT

Bakso Terong

2 servings

½ pound ground pork
   salt and pepper to taste
1 tablespoon chopped onion
1 teaspoon chopped garlic
1 medium egg
2 medium eggplants
½ cup water

Mix pork, salt, pepper, onion, garlic, and egg. Wash each
eggplant and cut a piece 1 inch thick off either end. Remove a
core about 1 inch in diameter from each eggplant. Fill cavities
with pork mixture. Place eggplants in a pan with the water.
Bring to a boil, reduce heat, and simmer ½ hour, or until eggplants are done. Cut in 1-inch-thick slices and serve with hot
sauce.*

Variation: STUFFED CUCUMBERS

Bakso Timun

2 servings

Follow same procedure as in Stuffed Eggplant, but replace eggplant with 2 large cucumbers.

MINCED PORK WITH GREEN BEANS

Babi Masak Buntjies

4 servings

½ pound chopped pork
1 medium onion, sliced
2 cloves garlic, sliced
2 tablespoons vegetable oil
salt and pepper to taste
½ cup water
1 cup diced green beans

Brown onion and garlic in oil. Add pork, salt, pepper, water, and green beans. Bring to a boil, reduce heat, and simmer 20 minutes, or until beans are tender. Serve hot.

Variation: MINCED PORK
WITH ASPARAGUS TIPS

Babi Masak Asperge

4 servings

Follow the same procedure as in Minced Pork with Green Beans, but replace green beans with 2 cups asparagus tips, cut diagonally in 1-inch pieces.

Cook asparagus only 3 minutes, in order to keep it crisp.

FRIED PORK WITH PEANUTS
Babi Masak Katjang Tanah

4 servings

½ pound pork, cubed
1 tablespoon soy sauce
1 tablespoon brown sugar
1 tablespoon flour
   salt and pepper to taste
1 cup vegetable oil
½ cup blanched peanuts

Toss meat with soy sauce, brown sugar, flour, salt, and pepper. Heat oil and fry meat until a crusty brown surface appears. Remove meat. Sauté peanuts for 10 minutes. Add pork and stir 3 minutes longer. Serve.

BARBECUED SPARERIBS I
Tulang Babi Panggang I

4 servings

2 pounds spareribs
½ cup soy sauce
¼ cup sherry
2 tablespoons brown sugar
½ cup pineapple juice
1 teaspoon ground ginger*
2 cloves garlic, minced
   salt and pepper to taste

Wash and separate ribs. Mix with remaining ingredients and marinate for 3 hours. Place ribs on a broiler rack and broil each side under low heat 20 minutes, basting each side with mixture.

BARBECUED SPARERIBS II
Tulang Babi Panggang II

4 servings

2 pounds spareribs
½ cup soy sauce
1 medium onion, chopped
2 cloves garlic, minced
1 tablespoon ground cinnamon
1 tablespoon sugar
1 tablespoon sherry
salt and pepper to taste
½ cup water

Wash and separate ribs. Rub with a mixture of remaining ingredients. Put in a pan, bring to a boil, reduce heat, and simmer until all liquid has been absorbed. Remove, place ribs on a broiler rack, and broil each side under low heat for 10 minutes.

PORK WITH SHINING NOODLES
AND VEGETABLES

Masak Kimlo

4 servings

½ cup shining noodles*
½ cup dried golden needles*
1 cup green beans,
    cut diagonally in 1-inch pieces
½ pound pork, cut into slivers
½ cup blanched peanuts
1 cup shredded white cabbage
½ cup cloud ears*
2 cups water
    salt and pepper to taste
½ cup fried crisp onion flakes (*see index*)

Soak shining noodles in water 2 minutes. Wash golden needles, remove hard stem, and slit soft part in half. Soak in water 2 minutes, drain. Add all ingredients, except onion flakes, to water. Bring to a boil, reduce heat, and simmer 40 minutes. Serve hot, with onion flakes on top.

SAUTÉED PORK WITH SHINING NOODLES

Babi Masak So-un

4 servings

2 large Chinese mushrooms*
2 cups shining noodles*
1 medium onion
2 tablespoons vegetable oil
¼ pound lean pork, cut into slivers
¼ pound shrimp, shelled and cooked

1 tablespoon sherry
1 tablespoon soy sauce
    salt and pepper to taste
½ cup stock
½ cup chopped celery

Soak mushrooms in water for 2 hours, then cut into slivers. Soak noodles in water for 2 minutes. Brown onion in oil. Add pork, shrimp, and sherry and stir quickly, until alcohol has evaporated (about 3 minutes). Add soy sauce, salt, pepper, stock, noodles, and mushrooms and heat thoroughly for 10 minutes. One minute before serving, add chopped celery.

SAUTÉED PORK KIDNEYS

Masak Jotjio

4 servings

5 pork kidneys
    salt
½ cup sherry
1 medium onion, sliced
3 cloves garlic, sliced
1 tablespoon ginger, cut julienne
2 tablespoons vegetable oil
¼ pound lean pork, cut into slivers
¼ pound pork liver, cut into slivers
2 tablespoons soy sauce
½ cup celery, cut julienne

Rub kidneys with a lot of salt, cut in halves, remove membranes, and core. Slash lightly with a sharp knife, making diamond patterns. Wash several times, then cut into 1-inch slices. Soak in sherry for 30 minutes. Brown onion and garlic in oil, then add ginger, liver, pork, kidneys with sherry, and soy sauce. Stir and simmer gently 30 minutes. One minute before serving, add celery. Serve hot.

SAUTÉED PORK LIVER

Masak Hati Babi

4 servings

1 pound pork liver
2 stalks leek, chopped
2 tablespoons vegetable oil
2 tablespoons soy sauce
1 tablespoon sherry
  salt and pepper to taste
2 stalks celery, cut julienne

Wash pork liver and cut into 1-inch slices. Brown leek in oil, then add liver, soy sauce, sherry, salt, and pepper. Simmer 6 minutes. One minute before serving, add celery. Serve piping hot.

STEAMED CHINESE SAUSAGE

Laktjang

4 servings

4 pair Chinese sausages*
1 cup mushrooms, sliced
  salt and pepper to taste

Wash sausage and cut diagonally in 1½-inch slices. Place on a plate, add mushrooms, salt, and pepper. Steam 30 minutes. Serve hot.

GRILLED CHINESE SAUSAGE

Laktjang Goreng

4 servings

4 pair Chinese sausages*

Wash sausages. Put into boiling water and cook 2 minutes. Remove quickly. Throw out water, heat skillet, and brown sausages, turning several times.

BRAISED BEEF WITH SOY SAUCE

Daging Semoor

4 servings

1 pound shank beef
½ stick butter (¼ cup)
1 medium onion, sliced
2 cloves garlic, sliced
1 cup water
2 tablespoons soy sauce
1 teaspoon ground cinnamon
    salt and pepper to taste

Wash beef and drain. Heat butter in a skillet and brown meat on both sides. Remove meat. Brown onion and garlic in rest of fat. Add beef, water, soy sauce, cinnamon, salt, and pepper and simmer 30 minutes. Cut meat in 1-inch slices, pour gravy over. Serve hot.

Variation 1: BRAISED BEEF
WITH SOY SAUCE AND POTATOES
Daging Semoor Pakai Kentang

4 servings

Follow same procedure as in Braised Beef with Soy Sauce, but cut meat in strips 1½ inches long by 1 inch wide before frying and add ½ pound quartered, medium-size potatoes to meat. Simmer 30 minutes and serve hot.

Variation 2: BRAISED BEEF
WITH SOY SAUCE AND CABBAGE
Semoor Daging Pakai Kol

4 servings

Follow same procedure as in Braised Beef with Soy Sauce, but add 2 cups shredded cabbage. Simmer until cabbage is tender. The cabbage will give a different taste to the meat.

BEEF WITH HOT RED PEPPERS
Sambal Gadang

6 servings

    2 pounds shank beef
    1 medium size onion, chopped
    3 tablespoons ground hot red pepper°
    ½ cup tamarind juice (*see index*) or lemon juice
    1 teaspoon turmeric°
    1 tablespoon paprika
      salt to taste
    2 cups water

Wash beef and drain. Rub with a mixture of onion, red pepper, tamarind juice, turmeric, paprika, and salt. Put in a pan, add water, and bring to a boil. Reduce heat and simmer 30 minutes, or until meat is tender. This dish can be served hot or cold, and may be kept in the refrigerator for several days.

BEEF CURRY

Kerie Daging

4 servings

1 pound shank beef
1 medium onion, sliced
2 cloves garlic, sliced
1 tablespoon vegetable oil
    salt to taste
1 tablespoon curry powder
1 teaspoon ground coriander
1 teaspoon ground caraway
1 cup diced green beans
½ cup shining noodles*
1 cup cabbage, cut in 1½-inch squares
2 cups coconut milk*

Wash beef, then cut in 1½-inch cubes. Brown onion and garlic in oil. Add beef, salt, curry powder and other spices, beans, shining noodles, cabbage, and coconut milk. Bring to a boil, reduce heat, and simmer, stirring constantly, for 20 minutes.

BARBECUED BEEF

Daging Panggang

4 servings

1½ pounds shank beef
1 teaspoon turmeric*
1 tablespoon ground hot red pepper*
salt to taste
½ cup melted butter (1 stick)
½ cup water

Wash beef and drain. Mix turmeric, red pepper, salt, butter, and water and rub on beef. Heat broiler to 350°. Place meat on the middle of the broiler rack, about 3 inches from the heating unit. Broil meat until the top side is well browned. Turn and broil until the second side is browned. (Turn meat only once.) Serve the meat on a platter, cut in ½-inch slices, with Peanut Butter Sauce (*see index*).

BRAISED BEEF WITH GINGER

Daging Masak Djahe

4 servings

1 pound shank beef, cut julienne
1 medium onion, sliced
2 cloves garlic, sliced
1 tablespoon vegetable oil
2 tablespoons ginger, cut julienne
2 tablespoons soy sauce
salt and pepper to taste
½ cup water
2 stalks celery, cut julienne

Wash beef and drain. Brown onion and garlic in oil. Add ginger and stir 1 minute. Add beef, soy sauce, salt, pepper, and water. Bring to a boil, reduce heat, and simmer 20 minutes, or until beef is tender. One minute before serving, add celery. Serve hot.

BRAISED BEEF WITH SALTED SOYBEANS
Daging Masak Taotjo

4 servings

1 tablespoon vegetable oil
1 medium onion, sliced
1 pound shank beef, cut julienne
2 tablespoons salted soybeans*
  salt to taste
2 cups coconut milk*
2 green peppers, cut julienne
2 stalks celery, cut julienne

Heat oil and brown onion. Add beef, soybeans, salt, and coconut milk. Bring to a boil, reduce heat, and simmer 20 minutes, or until beef is tender. Two minutes before serving, add green peppers and celery. Serve hot.

FRIED SHREDDED BEEF

Abon

6 servings

1½ pounds shank beef
2 cups water
½ cup tamarind juice (*see index*)
   salt and pepper to taste
2 cups vegetable oil

Stew beef 30 minutes in water. Remove beef and grate on a grater. Meat will fall in long fibers. Add salt, pepper, and tamarind juice to meat and fry in hot oil until light brown. Drain.

This meat can be kept in a jar, tightly closed to prevent loss of crispness.

BEEF WITH GRATED COCONUT

Dendeng Ragi

6 servings

1½ pounds shank beef
1½ cups grated coconut*
 ½ cup tamarind juice (*see index*)
1 bay leaf
1 teaspoon shrimp paste*
   salt to taste
2 cups vegetable oil

Wash beef, drain. Cut beef in 1½-inch cubes, put in a frying pan, and add all ingredients except oil. Bring to a boil, reduce heat, and simmer 20 minutes. Add oil, fry until light brown, and drain.

FRIED BEEF WITH SPICES
Empal Pedas

6 servings

1½ pounds shank beef
1 cup water
3 hot red peppers, crushed*
1 teaspoon ground caraway
2 teaspoons ground coriander
3 cloves garlic, crushed
½ teaspoon turmeric*
salt and pepper to taste
1 tablespoon sugar
½ cup tamarind juice (see index)
½ cup coconut milk*
2 cups vegetable oil

Stew beef in water for 15 minutes. Remove meat and cut in 1-inch slices. Mix hot peppers, caraway, coriander, garlic, turmeric, salt, pepper, sugar, tamarind juice, and coconut milk and add to liquid in the pan. Bring to a boil, add meat, and boil 15 minutes, or until all juice has been absorbed. Heat oil and deep fry meat until light brown. Drain on absorbent paper.

FRIED BEEF WITH TAMARIND JUICE

Empal Daging

6 servings

1½ pounds shank beef
1 cup water
½ cup tamarind juice (*see index*)
  salt and pepper to taste
2 cups vegetable oil

Stew beef for 15 minutes in water. Remove and cut in slices 1 inch thick. Return to the pan, and add tamarind juice, salt, and pepper. Boil 5 minutes, turning several times in order to let meat absorb tamarind juice. Heat oil and fry meat until light brown.

FRIED BEEF WITH RED PEPPER

Dendeng Lambok

6 servings

2 pounds shank beef
½ cup tamarind juice (*see index*) or lemon juice
  salt and pepper to taste
1 cup vegetable oil
2 medium onions, sliced
1 cup diagonally sliced hot red peppers*
1 teaspoon shrimp paste*
2 tablespoons vinegar

Cut beef in strips 1½ inches long by 1 inch wide. Wash and drain, mix with tamarind juice, salt, and pepper. Bring to a boil, reduce heat, and simmer 20 minutes, or until meat is just underdone. Add oil and fry until light brown. Remove meat and add onions, red peppers, and shrimp paste dissolved in vinegar. Stir 2 minutes. Add beef to mixture and stir 1 minute. Serve hot or cold.

CRISP BEEF WITH HOT RED PEPPER
Dendeng Belado

6 servings

1½ pounds shank beef
½ cup tamarind juice (*see index*)
   salt and pepper to taste
1 tablespoon ground ginger
1 tablespoon ground caraway
1 tablespoon ground coriander
2 cups vegetable oil
½ cup ground hot red peppers *
1 medium onion, minced
2 tablespoons vinegar

Slice beef, as thin as possible, into large pieces. Wash, drain, and mix with tamarind juice, salt, pepper, ginger, caraway, and coriander. Marinate 1 hour and drain. Heat oven to 350° and roast meat until dry (about 40 minutes). Cut into 2-inch squares and fry in oil until crisp. Remove oil from frying pan, leaving only 1 tablespoon. Add red pepper and onion and fry 5 minutes, then add vinegar and stir 3 minutes. Add crisp meat, mix, and serve.

This meat can be kept in a jar, tightly closed to prevent loss of crispness.

BEEF WITH COCONUT BUTTER

Rendang Pandang

8 servings

2 pounds shank beef
2 cups coconut milk*
3 tablespoons coconut butter (see index)
1 tablespoon ground hot red pepper*
½ tablespoon turmeric*
10 mint leaves
    salt to taste
1 medium onion, ground
2 cloves garlic, ground
½ cup tamarind juice (see index)
1 cup vegetable oil

Cut beef in 1½-inch cubes. Wash, drain, and put in a frying pan. Add all other ingredients except oil. Bring to a boil, then cook on moderate heat for about 25 minutes, or until all liquid has been absorbed. Add oil and fry, constantly stirring, until mixture is light brown.

This dish can be kept several days in the refrigerator, but should be heated before serving.

Variation 1: BEEF WITH COCONUT MILK

Gulai Kelio

8 servings

Follow same procedure as in Beef with Coconut Butter, but use 3 cups of coconut milk* instead of oil. When meat is done, there should be a thick sauce of coconut left.

Variation 2: BEEF LIVER WITH COCONUT MILK

Gulai Kelio Hati

8 servings

Follow same procedure as in Beef with Coconut Butter, but substitute 3 cups of coconut milk° for the oil and 2 pounds of beef liver, cut in 1½-inch cubes, for the beef. When liver is done, there should be a thick sauce of coconut left.

FRIED SPICED BEEF

Terik

6 servings

1½ pounds shank beef
    salt and pepper to taste
1 teaspoon shrimp paste°
1 tablespoon tamarind juice (*see index*)
1 tablespoon ground coriander
1 teaspoon ground caraway
2 cups vegetable oil

Cut beef in 1-inch cubes. Wash and drain. Put into a pan, with all ingredients except oil. Bring to a boil, reduce heat, and simmer 20 minutes, or until all liquid has been absorbed by the beef. Add oil and fry until light brown.

STEWED BEEF WITH BROTH

Soto Daging

6 servings

1 pound shank beef
1 tablespoon vegetable oil
1 large onion, chopped
3 cloves garlic, chopped
1 teaspoon shrimp paste*
2 slices ginger (*see index*)
½ teaspoon turmeric*
   salt and pepper to taste
½ cup diced scallion
2 hard-cooked eggs, sliced
½ cup fried crisp onion flakes (*see index*)

Cut beef in strips 1½ inches long by 1 inch wide. Wash, and put in a pan, and add water to cover. Bring to a boil, reduce heat, and simmer 20 minutes. Heat oil and brown onion and garlic. Add shrimp paste, ginger, turmeric, beef, stock, salt, pepper, and scallion. Cook 10 minutes longer. Serve hot, with sliced eggs and onion flakes on top. Serve soy sauce and hot sauce* on the side.

Variation 1: STEWED BEEF WITH BROTH

MADURA STYLE[1]
Soto Madura

6 servings

Follow same procedure as in Stewed Beef with Broth, but use only ½ pound of shank beef and add 1 pound of sliced beef tripe. Cook for 1 hour to allow tripe to become tender. Substitute 2 stalks of chopped celery for the sliced eggs.

---

[1] Madura is an island east of Java.

Variation 2: STEWED TRIPE WITH BROTH

Soto Babat

6 servings

Follow same procedure as Stewed Beef with Broth, but replace beef with 2 pounds of sliced beef tripe. Permit tripe to cook 1 hour or more, until tender.

BRAISED BEEF WITH COCONUT BUTTER

Gulai Masak Pedes

6 servings

1½ pounds shank beef
1 tablespoon vegetable oil
2 tablespoons ground hot red pepper*
1 teaspoon turmeric*
1 tablespoon coconut butter (*see index*)
  salt to taste
2 cups water

Cut beef in 1-inch cubes, then wash and drain. Heat oil and brown red pepper. Add turmeric, beef, coconut butter, salt, and water. Simmer 30 minutes, or until beef is tender.

BRAISED BEEF IN BUTTER SAUCE
Gulai Lapis

6 servings

1½ pounds shank beef
 1 teaspoon ground cinnamon
  salt and pepper to taste
 ½ cup bread crumbs
 1 stick butter (½ cup butter)
 1 large onion, chopped
 2 cups water
 2 tablespoons soy sauce

Cut beef in slices 1 inch thick, then wash and drain. Mix beef with cinnamon, salt, and pepper. Cover each meat slice with bread crumbs and fry in butter until light brown. Add onion and stir 2 minutes. Add water and soy sauce and simmer until meat is tender, about 20–30 minutes.

BRAISED BEEF WITH SPICES
Besengek Daging

6 servings

1½ pounds shank beef
 2 tablespoons vegetable oil
 1 large onion, sliced
 2 cloves garlic, sliced
 2 tablespoons brown sugar
 ¼ cup tamarind juice (*see index*)
  salt and pepper to taste
 2 bay leaves
 1 teaspoon ground coriander
 1 teaspoon ground caraway
 2 hot red peppers, sliced diagonally*

Cut beef in strips 1½ inches long by 1 inch wide. Heat oil and brown onion and garlic. Add beef and all other ingredients. Bring to a boil, reduce heat, and simmer gently for 20–30 minutes, or until meat is tender.

BRAISED BEEF WITH CABBAGE

Pindang Daging Dengan Kol

4 servings

1 pound shank beef
4 hot red peppers, sliced diagonally*
2 cloves garlic, sliced
1 medium onion, sliced
1 teaspoon shrimp paste*
  salt to taste
1 tablespoon sugar
2 tablespoons soy sauce
1 tablespoon tamarind juice (*see index*)
2 cups water

Cut beef in 1-inch cubes, then wash and put in a pan. Add all other ingredients and bring to a boil. Reduce heat and simmer 20–30 minutes, or until beef is tender.

BEEFSTEAK JAVANESE STYLE

Bifstik Djawa

6 servings

2 pounds beef
1 medium onion, chopped
2 cloves garlic, chopped
  salt and pepper to taste
1 teaspoon ground nutmeg
1 stick butter (½ cup)
2 cups water

Wash beef, then dry. Mix onion, garlic, salt, pepper, and nutmeg. Rub beef with this mixture. Let stand ½ hour to allow spices to penetrate the meat. Heat butter and brown meat. Add water and bring to a boil. Reduce heat and simmer 30 minutes, or until meat is done. With a sharp knife, cut slices ½ inch thick. Serve meat with gravy poured over.

BRAISED BEEF

Bumbu Rudjak Daging

6 servings

1½ pounds shank beef
1 large onion, chopped
2 cloves garlic, chopped
1 tablespoon vegetable oil
1 cup coconut milk*
2 hot red peppers, diagonally sliced*
1 teaspoon shrimp paste*
1 tablespoon tamarind juice (see index)
  salt and pepper to taste

Wash beef and cut in 1-inch cubes. Brown onion and garlic in oil, then add beef and all other ingredients. Simmer 20–30 minutes, or until beef is tender.

BRAISED BEEF WITH SPICES

Gulai Bagar

6 servings

1½ pounds shank beef
1 tablespoon vegetable oil
1 large onion, sliced
2 cloves garlic, sliced
3 tablespoons ground hot red pepper*
1 teaspoon turmeric*
1 tablespoon paprika
1 tablespoon ground coriander
1 teaspoon ground caraway
1 teaspoon ground ginger*
5 whole cloves
1 2-inch piece cinnamon stick
   salt to taste
2 cups coconut milk*
1 pound medium potatoes, peeled and quartered

Cut beef in strips 1 inch by 1½ inches, wash and drain. Heat oil and brown onion and garlic. Add beef, all spices, coconut milk, and potatoes. Bring to a boil, reduce heat, and simmer 30 minutes, or until meat and potatoes are tender.

Variation 1: BRAISED BEEF WITH SPICES AND EGGPLANT

Gulai Bagar Terong

6 servings

Follow same procedure as in Braised Beef with Spices, but replace potatoes with 2 medium eggplants, cut in 1½-inch cubes.

Variation 2: BRAISED BEEF
WITH SPICES IN TURMERIC SAUCE

Gulai Korma

6 servings

Follow same procedure as in Braised Beef with Spices, but omit hot red peppers and use 1 tablespoon turmeric* instead of 1 teaspoon.

BRAISED BEEF WITH LIVER

Pindang Daging Hati

6 servings

1½ pounds shank beef
1 pound beef liver
4 hot red peppers, split*
1 medium onion, sliced
5 cloves garlic, sliced
1 tablespoon tamarind juice (*see index*)
2 tablespoons soy sauce
1 teaspoon turmeric*
salt and pepper to taste
3 cups water

Cut beef and liver in 1½-inch cubes, then wash and drain. Put in a pan and add all other ingredients. Bring to a boil, reduce heat, and simmer 40 minutes, or until meat and liver are tender.

BEEF IN BROWN SAUCE

Hache, Aseh

6 servings

1½ pounds shank beef
1 large onion, sliced
1 stick butter (½ cup)
  salt and pepper to taste
1 tablespoon soy sauce
1 tablespoon vinegar
2 cups water
5 whole cloves
1 tablespoon flour

Cut beef in ½-inch cubes, then wash and drain. Brown onion in butter. Add beef and all other ingredients except flour. Bring to a boil, reduce heat, and simmer 30 minutes, or until meat is tender. Three minutes before serving, add flour. Serve hot.

FRIED BEEF TRIPE

Babat Goreng

6 servings

1½ pounds beef tripe
½ cup tamarind juice (*see index*)
  salt to taste
2 cups vegetable oil

Cut tripe in 2-inch squares, put in a pan, add water enough to cover, and simmer 1 hour, or until tripe is tender. Drain off water. Add tamarind juice and salt and simmer 5 minutes longer. Take out tripe and fry it in hot oil until golden brown.

SAUTÉED TRIPE

Babat Tumis

6 servings

1½ pounds honeycomb tripe
3 tablespoons vegetable oil
2 small onions, sliced
1 tablespoon ginger, cut julienne*
3 cloves garlic, sliced
1 tablespoon sherry
  salt and pepper to taste
½ cup fried crisp onion flakes (*see index*)

Cut tripe in 1-inch slices. Heat oil in a skillet and brown onion, ginger, and garlic. Increase heat. When oil is very hot, add tripe. Stir immediately, maintaining heat in order to make tripe slices curl. Simmer 5 minutes, then add sherry, salt, and pepper. Cook 5 minutes longer. Serve hot, with onion flakes on top.

TRIPE WITH COCONUT MILK

Babat Masak Kelapa

6 servings

1½ pounds tripe
1 tablespoon ground hot red pepper*
½ teaspoon turmeric*
1 teaspoon paprika
  salt to taste
5 mint leaves
2 cups coconut milk*

Cut tripe into 2-inch squares. Put in a pan, add red pepper, turmeric, paprika, salt, mint leaves, and water to cover. Bring to a boil, reduce heat, and simmer 1 hour, or until tripe is tender. Add coconut milk and cook 5 minutes longer.

TRIPE WITH HOT RED PEPPER
Babat Masak Goreng Asam

6 servings

1½ pounds tripe
1 tablespoon vegetable oil
1 large onion, sliced
3 tablespoons ground hot red pepper*
1 teaspoon paprika
  salt to taste
5 mint leaves
1 teaspoon shrimp paste*
2 cups tamarind juice (*see index*)

Cut tripe into 1½-inch slices. Heat oil and brown onion. Add tripe and all other ingredients. Bring to a boil, reduce heat, and simmer gently for 1 hour or until tripe is tender.

Variation 1: HEART WITH HOT RED PEPPER

Djantung Masak Goreng Asam

4 servings

Follow same procedure as in Tripe with Hot Red Pepper, but replace tripe with 1 pound of beef heart, cut in 1-inch slices. Simmer 30 minutes instead of 1 hour.

Variation 2: LIVER WITH HOT RED PEPPER

Hati Masak Goreng Asam

4 servings

Follow same procedure as in Tripe with Hot Red Pepper, but replace tripe with 1 pound of beef liver, cut in 2-inch cubes. Cook only 30 minutes instead of 1 hour.

FRIED BEEF LIVER
Hati Goreng

6 servings

1½ pounds beef liver
1 cup water
  salt and pepper to taste
1 teaspoon ground caraway
1 tablespoon ground coriander
½ cup tamarind juice (*see index*)
2 cups vegetable oil

Cut liver in 1½-inch cubes, then wash several times and drain. Put in a pan and add water, salt, pepper, caraway, and coriander. Bring to a boil, reduce heat, and simmer 30 minutes, or until liver is well done. Add tamarind juice and cook 15 minutes longer on a high heat, until all juice has been absorbed. Fry in hot oil until light brown.

Variation: FRIED BEEF HEART

Dendeng Djantung

4 servings

Follow same procedure as in Fried Beef Liver, but replace liver with 1 pound beef heart, cut in 2-inch squares.

CALF'S BRAINS IN COCONUT MILK
Gulai Otak

4 servings

1 pound calf's brains
1 tablespoon oil
1 small onion, chopped

1 tablespoon ground hot red pepper*
½ teaspoon turmeric*
1 cup coconut milk*
  salt to taste
5 mint leaves

Soak brains in salted water for 10 minutes. Remove, put into boiling water, and cook for 5 minutes. Drain, remove membrane, and cut into 3-inch cubes. Heat oil and brown onion. Add red pepper, turmeric, coconut milk, salt, mint leaves, and brain. Bring to a boil, reduce heat, and simmer 20 minutes.

FRIED CALF'S BRAIN WITH HAM
Otak Goreng Gulung Ham

6 servings

1½ pounds calf's brains
½ cup flour
½ cup water
1 large egg
1 teaspoon baking powder
1 pound Smithfield ham,
  cut in strips 1½ inches long by 1 inch wide
  salt and pepper to taste
2 cups vegetable oil

Soak brains in salted water for 10 minutes. Remove, put into boiling water, and cook for 5 minutes. Drain, remove membrane, and cut in 1½-inch slices. Make a batter from flour, water, egg, baking powder, salt, and pepper. Roll each brain slice in a slice of ham, dip in batter, and fry in hot oil until light brown. Drain on absorbent paper and serve.

Variation: FRIED CALF'S BRAINS WITH BACON

Otak Goreng Gulung Spek

6 servings

Follow same procedure as in Fried Calf's Brain with Ham, but replace ham with 1 pound of bacon strips.

MARINATED CALF'S BRAINS

Otak Tjuka

6 servings

1½ pounds calf's brains
  1 cup vinegar
    salt and pepper to taste
  2 bay leaves
  3 cloves garlic, whole
  1 small onion, sliced

Soak brains in salted water for 10 minutes. Remove, put into boiling water, and cook for 5 minutes. Drain, remove membrane, and cut in 2-inch slices. Pour vinegar in a pan and add all other ingredients. Bring to a boil, reduce heat, and add brains. Simmer 5 minutes longer. Keep overnight before serving. Serve cold.

 # POULTRY

STUFFED CHICKEN I
Ajam Liong Kee

6 servings

1 3–3½-pound chicken
4 Chinese mushrooms *
½ pound pork, ground
1 small onion, chopped
1 clove garlic, chopped
½ pound Smithfield ham, chopped
½ cup fried crisp onion flakes (*see index*)
2 medium eggs
2 tablespoons chopped celery
1 tablespoon soy sauce
   salt and pepper to taste

Soak mushrooms in water for 2 hours, then slice. Wash chicken inside and out and drain. Mix pork with all other ingredients. Stuff cavity of chicken with pork mixture and sew up opening. Put chicken in boiling water to cover, reduce heat, and simmer 1½ hours. Turn once or twice during cooking. Serve chicken hot, with gravy poured over.

STUFFED CHICKEN II

Ajam Kodok

6 servings

1 3–3½-pound chicken
2 small potatoes
1 stick butter (½ cup)
1 large onion, sliced
3 cloves garlic, sliced
1 cup sliced chicken hearts, livers, and gizzards
1 tablespoon soy sauce
1 teaspoon ground cinnamon
  salt and pepper to taste
3 cups water

Wash chicken inside and out and drain. Peel potatoes and cut in ½-inch-wide sticks. Heat half of the butter and brown onion and garlic. Add hearts, livers, gizzards, soy sauce, cinnamon, salt, pepper, and potatoes. Simmer 10 minutes. Stuff cavity of chicken with this mixture and sew up opening. Heat rest of butter and brown chicken, turning several times. Add water and bring to a boil. Reduce heat and simmer until chicken is tender, about 40 minutes. Serve chicken hot, pouring gravy over.

CHICKEN STUFFED WITH CHESTNUTS

Ajam Isi Kastanje

6 servings

1 3–3½-pound chicken
½ pound chestnuts, boiled
1 small onion, sliced
1 stick butter (½ cup)
½ cup chopped Smithfield ham
½ cup mashed potatoes
  salt and pepper to taste

Wash chicken inside and out and drain. Peel and chop chestnuts. Brown onion in butter, add ham and all other ingredients. Stir for 5 minutes. Remove from heat and cool. Stuff chicken cavity with this mixture and sew up opening. Heat oven to 300°. Put chicken in roasting pan and roast for 2 hours.

CHICKEN STUFFED WITH HAM AND EGGS

Ajam Isi Ham Dan Telur

6 servings

1 3–3½ -pound chicken
½ pound pork, chopped
1 teaspoon ground cinnamon
   salt and pepper to taste
1 small onion, chopped
2 cloves garlic, chopped
3 small eggs, hard-cooked
2 4-inch dill pickles
¼ pound Smithfield ham, cut in strips 2½ inches
   long by 1 inch wide

Wash chicken inside and out and drain. Mix pork with cinnamon, salt, pepper, onion, and garlic. Shell eggs and cut in half. Slice pickles lengthwise. Fill chicken cavity thus: Start with layer of pork. On top place a layer of egg halves, then ham and pickle slices. Sew up opening. Put chicken in roasting pan in 300° oven and roast for 2 hours.

CHICKEN STUFFED WITH
FRESH MUSHROOMS
Ajam Isi Djamur

6 servings

1 3–3½ -pound chicken
1 medium onion, sliced
3 cloves garlic, sliced
1 stick butter (½ cup)
1 pound fresh mushrooms, sliced
  salt and pepper to taste

Wash chicken inside and out and drain. Brown onion and garlic in butter, and add mushrooms, salt, and pepper. Cook 5 minutes. Stuff chicken cavity with this mixture and sew up opening. Put chicken in boiling water, reduce heat, and simmer 40 minutes, or until meat is tender.

CHICKEN STUFFED WITH BIRD'S-NEST
Ajam Isi Sarang Burung

4 servings

1 1½ –2 pound chicken
1 cup bird's-nest*
½ cup chopped Smithfield ham
¼ cup chopped celery
3 slices ginger (*see index*)
  salt and pepper to taste

Wash chicken inside and out and drain. Soak bird's-nest in water 3 hours. Drain bird's-nest and mix with ham, celery, and pepper. Stuff chicken cavity with mixture and sew up opening. Put chicken in boiling water to cover. Add ginger and salt. Reduce heat and simmer 1 hour, or until chicken is tender. Serve hot.

FRIED CHICKEN
Ajam Goreng Asem

4 servings

1 2–2½ pound chicken
2 cups water
½ cup tamarind juice (*see index*)
   salt to taste
2 cups vegetable oil

Cut chicken in pieces. Boil the water, put in chicken pieces and simmer 10 minutes. Strain, reserving stock for future use. Add tamarind juice and salt to chicken pieces and boil 5 minutes. Heat oil and fry chicken to light brown color.

FRIED CHICKEN WITH HOT RED PEPPER
Ajam Belado

4 servings

1 2½–3-pound chicken
   salt to taste
1½ cups vegetable oil
2 medium onions, chopped
½ cup chopped hot red peppers*
2 tablespoons lemon juice

Cut chicken in pieces, rub with salt, and let stand 10 minutes. Put in a frying pan and cover with water. Bring to a boil, reduce heat, and simmer 10 minutes. Remove chicken and drain. Fry in hot oil (375°) until light brown, about 8 minutes. Remove oil, leaving 2 tablespoons in pan. Brown onion. Add red peppers and stir 2 minutes. Add lemon juice, stir 2 minutes longer, add chicken, and mix until all parts of chicken are covered with red pepper.

FRIED CHICKEN WITH SPICES

Ajam Goreng Djawa

4 servings

1 2–2½ -pound chicken
2 hot red peppers, split*
1 small onion, sliced
2 teaspoons ground coriander
1 teaspoon ground caraway
    salt to taste
1 teaspoon turmeric*
2 tablespoons tamarind juice (*see index*)
2 tablespoons brown sugar
1 cup coconut milk*
2 cups vegetable oil

Cut chicken in sections, then wash and drain. Put in a pan and add all other ingredients, except oil. Bring to a boil, reduce heat, and simmer 20 minutes, or until liquid has been absorbed. Heat oil and deep fry chicken until golden brown. Drain on absorbent paper.

BROILED CHICKEN WITH COCONUT MILK

Ajam Panggang Santan

4 servings

1 2–2½ -pound chicken
2 cups coconut milk*
1 tablespoon ground hot red pepper*

1 medium onion, chopped
    salt to taste
1 teaspoon turmeric*
5 mint leaves

Wash chicken, then split in half and drain. Put in a pan and add all other ingredients. Bring to a boil, reduce heat, and simmer 20 minutes, or until all liquid has evaporated and only a thick sauce remains. Remove chicken and keep sauce warm. Broil chicken pieces under medium heat 30 minutes. Serve with the sauce on top.

BROILED CHICKEN WITH SOY SAUCE
Ajam Panggang Ketjap

4 servings

1 2–2½ pound chicken
2 tablespoons soy sauce
    salt and pepper to taste
½ cup water
1 tablespoon lemon juice
1 tablespoon ground hot red pepper*
1 stick butter (½ cup)

Wash chicken, split in half, and drain. Put in a pan, add soy sauce, salt, pepper, and water. Bring to a boil, reduce heat, and simmer 10 minutes. Remove chicken and broil 30 minutes under moderate heat. Add lemon juice, butter, and hot pepper to chicken stock, and pour over chicken. Serve.

BROILED CHICKEN WITH SPICES I
Ajam Panggang Bumbu Besengek

4 servings

1 2–2½-pound chicken
1 tablespoon vegetable oil
1 medium onion, chopped
2 cloves garlic, chopped
1 tablespoon ground hot red pepper*
1 teaspoon shrimp paste*
2 cups coconut milk*
2 tablespoons tamarind juice (*see index*)
1 tablespoon brown sugar
1 teaspoon ground coriander
1 teaspoon ground caraway

Wash chicken, then drain and cut in half. Heat oil and brown onion and garlic, then add chicken and all other ingredients. Bring to a boil, reduce heat, and simmer 20 minutes, or until all liquid has evaporated and only a thick sauce remains. Broil chicken 30 minutes under medium heat. Serve with the sauce on top.

BROILED CHICKEN WITH SPICES II
Ajam Panggang Bumbu Rudjak

4 servings

1 2–2½-pound chicken
1 medium onion, chopped
2 cloves garlic, chopped

1 tablespoon vegetable oil
2 tablespoons ground hot red pepper*
1 teaspoon shrimp paste*
1 tablespoon tamarind juice (*see index*)
  salt to taste

Wash chicken, then drain and split in half. Brown onion and garlic in oil. Add chicken and remaining ingredients. Bring to a boil and simmer 20 minutes. Keeping sauce warm, remove chicken and broil 30 minutes under medium heat. Pour sauce over chicken. Serve.

BROILED CHICKEN WITH SPICES III

Ajam Panggang Bumbu Kuning

4 servings

1 2–2½-pound chicken
1 tablespoon ground nuts
1 medium onion, chopped
2 cloves garlic, chopped
1 tablespoon ground coriander
1 teaspoon ground caraway
1 teaspoon shrimp paste*
  salt and pepper to taste
1 cup coconut milk*
1 tablespoon turmeric*

Wash chicken, drain and split in half. Put in a pan, add all ingredients, and bring to a boil. Reduce heat and simmer 20 minutes. Keeping sauce warm, remove chicken and broil 30 minutes under medium heat. Pour sauce over chicken. Serve.

BRAISED CHICKEN JAVANESE STYLE I
Ajam Semoor Djawa

4 servings

1 2–2½-pound chicken
2 tablespoons tamarind juice (*see index*)
  salt to taste
½ cup vegetable oil
1 medium onion, sliced
1 clove garlic, sliced
3 hot red peppers, sliced diagonally*
1 tablespoon brown sugar
1 tablespoon vinegar
5 whole peppercorns
2 cups water

Wash chicken, then cut in pieces and rub with tamarind juice and salt. Brown in oil. Remove and brown onion and garlic in remaining oil. Add remaining ingredients and chicken. Bring to a boil, reduce heat, and simmer 30 minutes, or until meat is tender.

BRAISED CHICKEN JAVANESE STYLE II
Ajam Opor

4 servings

1 2–2½-pound chicken
1 cup coconut milk*
2 hot red peppers, ground*
1 medium onion, chopped
2 cloves garlic, chopped
1 tablespoon sugar
  salt to taste

1 tablespoon ground coriander
1 teaspoon ground caraway
1 tablespoon lemon juice

Wash chicken, then drain and split in half. Broil 20 minutes under moderate heat. Cut in pieces. Heat coconut milk, and add remaining ingredients and chicken. Bring to a boil, reduce heat, and simmer 30 minutes. Serve.

BRAISED CHICKEN JAVANESE STYLE III

Ajam Lambarang

4 servings

1 2–2½ -pound chicken
   salt to taste
1 tablespoon vegetable oil
1 medium onion, sliced
2 cloves garlic, sliced
½ teaspoon turmeric*
1 tablespoon ground coriander
1 teaspoon ground caraway
1 teaspoon shrimp paste*
2 cups coconut milk*
1 bay leaf

Wash chicken, then drain and cut in pieces. Rub with salt and let stand 20 minutes. Heat oil and brown onion and garlic. Add remaining ingredients and chicken. Bring to a boil, reduce heat, and simmer 30 minutes, or until meat is tender. Serve.

BRAISED CHICKEN MINAHASSA STYLE I[1]
Ajam Isi Di Bulu

4 servings

1 2–2½-pound chicken
salt and pepper to taste
3 medium tomatoes, cut in wedges
1 medium onion, chopped
2 tablespoons ground hot red pepper*
1 tablespoon chopped green pepper
½ cup chopped scallion
1 cup water

Wash chicken, then cut in pieces and rub with salt and pepper. Put in a pan and add tomato wedges and all other ingredients. Bring to a boil, reduce heat, and simmer 40 minutes, or until meat is tender.

(*Note:* According to the original recipe, chicken and all other ingredients are placed in a bamboo container [*bulu* means bamboo] and roasted above a charcoal fire, turning several times, until meat is tender.)

BRAISED CHICKEN MINAHASSA STYLE II[1]
Ajam Panike

4 servings

1 2–2½-pound chicken
½ cup vegetable oil
1 medium onion, chopped

[1] Minahassa is the northern part of Celebes.

        4 cloves garlic, chopped
        2 tablespoons ground hot red pepper*
        1 tablespoon shrimp paste*
        1 tablespoon tamarind juice (*see index*)
        1 tablespoon sugar
        ½ cup chopped nuts
        2 cups coconut milk*
        1 teaspoon ground ginger*
        salt to taste

Wash chicken, then cut in pieces and drain. Brown in hot oil. Remove chicken, then remove oil, leaving 1 tablespoon in pan. Brown onion, garlic, and red pepper in oil, then add chicken and remaining ingredients. Bring to a boil, reduce heat, and simmer 40 minutes, or until meat is tender.

FRIED CHICKEN MINAHASSA STYLE[1]

Ajam Goreng Ritja-Ritja

4 servings

        1 2–2½-pound chicken
        salt and pepper to taste
        1 cup vegetable oil
        1 medium onion, sliced
        1 tablespoon ground ginger*
        2 tablespoons ground hot red pepper*
        ½ cup water
        1 tablespoon vinegar

Wash chicken, then cut in pieces and rub with salt and pepper. Fry in hot oil until golden brown, remove, and drain. Remove oil, leaving 1 tablespoon in pan. Fry onion, ginger, and red pepper until light brown. Add water, vinegar, and chicken. Bring to a boil, reduce heat, and simmer 40 minutes, or until meat is tender.

[1] Minahassa is the northern part of Celebes.

BRAISED CHICKEN IN COCONUT MILK MINAHASSA STYLE[1]

Ajam Masak Tuturuga

4 servings

1 2–2½ -pound chicken
2 tablespoons oil
1 medium onion, chopped
1 tablespoon ground hot red pepper*
1 tablespoon turmeric*
½ cup ground nuts
    salt and pepper to taste
2 cups coconut milk*
1 tablespoon lemon juice

Wash chicken, then cut in pieces and drain. Heat oil and brown onion, red pepper, turmeric, and nuts. Add chicken and remaining ingredients. Bring to a boil, reduce heat, and simmer 30 minutes, or until meat is tender.

(*Note:* According to the original recipe turtle meat is used [*tuturuga* means turtle]. But any other kind of meat, duck, chicken, or beef, can be prepared in this way.)

CHICKEN CURRY

Ajam Kerie

4 servings

1 2–2½ -pound chicken
1 medium onion, sliced
2 cloves garlic, sliced

[1] Minahassa is the northern part of Celebes.

1 tablespoon vegetable oil
1 tablespoon curry powder*
1 tablespoon ground coriander
1 teaspoon ground caraway
   salt to taste
2 cups coconut milk*

Wash chicken, then cut in pieces and drain. Heat oil, brown onion and garlic. Add chicken and remaining ingredients. Bring to a boil, reduce heat, and simmer 40 minutes, or until meat is tender. Serve.

CHICKEN WITH COCONUT MILK

Ajam Pukang

4 servings

1 2–2½-pound chicken
1 medium onion, chopped
1 tablespoon vegetable oil
2 tablespoons ground hot red pepper*
1 tablespoon ground nuts
1 tablespoon ground coriander
1 teaspoon ground caraway
   salt to taste
2 cups coconut milk*
1 tablespoon tamarind juice (*see index*)

Wash chicken, then split in half and drain. Brown in broiler. Cut in pieces and bruise lightly with a rolling pin. Heat oil and brown onion. Add red pepper, nuts, chicken, and all other ingredients. Bring to a boil, reduce heat, and simmer 30 minutes, stirring occasionally. Serve.

CHICKEN WITH MUSHROOMS AND ALMONDS

Ajam Masak Djamur Dan Amandel

4 servings

1 chicken breast
1 medium onion, sliced
3 cloves garlic, sliced
1 tablespoon vegetable oil
½ cup blanched almonds
2 tablespoons soy sauce
½ cup water
1 tablespoon flour,
   dissolved in 2 tablespoons water

Slice meat from chicken breast. Brown onion and garlic in oil. Add chicken and all other ingredients except flour paste. Bring to a boil, reduce heat, and simmer 20 minutes. Add flour paste and simmer 5 minutes longer. Serve hot.

SLICED CHICKEN
IN SWEET-AND-SOUR SAUCE
Bong Tjha Kee

4 servings

2 chicken breasts, boned
1 large egg, beaten
3 tablespoons cornstarch
1 cup vegetable oil
1 medium onion, sliced
1 large tomato, sliced
½ cup sliced carrots
2 tablespoons sugar
salt and pepper to taste
2 tablespoons vinegar
½ cup water
1 cup sliced cauliflower
½ cup snow peas*

Cut chicken into slices ½ inch thick. Dip in beaten egg and then in cornstarch. Brown in oil, then remove and drain. Remove oil, leaving 1 tablespoon in pan. Brown onion in oil, then add tomato, carrots, sugar, salt, pepper, vinegar, and water. Bring to a boil, reduce heat, and simmer 10 minutes. Add chicken, cauliflower, and snow peas and simmer 2 minutes. Serve hot. (The sauce should taste sweet-sour.)

SWEET-AND-SOUR CHICKEN LIVERS

Hati Ajam Asem Manis

4 servings

>1 pound chicken livers, gizzards, and hearts
>1 medium cucumber
>1 medium carrot
>1 stalk celery
>1 tablespoon salt
>2 tablespoons vinegar
>2 tablespoons sugar
>3 slices ginger (*see index*)
>2 cloves garlic, sliced
>½ cup water
>1 tablespoon vegetable oil
>1 teaspoon cornstarch,
>   dissolved in 1 tablespoon water
>1 tablespoon soy sauce

Cut cucumber lengthwise, remove seeds, and cut diagonally in slices 1 inch thick. Cut carrot and celery diagonally in slices 1 inch thick. Rub celery, carrot, and cucumber with the salt and allow to stand 10 minutes. Pour off juice and add vinegar and sugar. Marinate 20 minutes, then drain. Brown ginger and garlic in oil. Add livers, hearts, gizzards, and water and bring to a boil. Reduce heat and simmer 20 minutes. Add cornstarch-water mixture, then add vegetables and simmer 5 minutes longer. Serve hot.

CHICKEN LIVERS WITH VEGETABLES

Kee Pak Lay Tjha

4 servings

>1 cup sliced gizzards
>1 cup sliced chicken livers

1 tablespoon cornstarch
½ cup vegetable oil
3 stalks Chinese leek*
½ cup sliced bamboo shoots*
½ cup sliced carrots
2 tablespoons sugar
  salt and pepper to taste
1 cup chicken stock
½ cup sliced cabbage
½ cup snow peas*
½ cup fried crisp onion flakes (*see index*)

Mix gizzards and livers with cornstarch. Brown in oil. Remove oil, leaving 1 tablespoon in pan. Cut leek in 2-inch slices and fry in oil. Add bamboo shoots, carrots, sugar, salt, pepper, gizzards, livers, and stock. Bring to a boil, reduce heat, and simmer 30 minutes. Add cabbage and snow peas and simmer 2 minutes longer. Serve, with onion flakes on top.

CHICKEN WITH PINEAPPLE

Ajam Masak Nanas

4 servings

2 chicken breasts, boned
1 tablespoon cornstarch
  salt and pepper to taste
1 tablespoon vegetable oil
1 clove garlic, sliced
1 cup pineapple wedges, fresh or canned
1 tablespoon soy sauce
½ cup water

Cut chicken in slices 1 inch thick. Mix with cornstarch, salt, and pepper. Fry in hot oil until just underdone, about 5 minutes. Add garlic and pineapple and simmer 5 minutes. Add soy sauce and water and simmer 5 minutes longer. Serve hot.

CHICKEN WITH CHESTNUTS

Ajam Masak Kastanje

4 servings

½ pound chestnuts
1 1½–2-pound chicken
1 tablespoon sherry
2 tablespoons soy sauce
1 tablespoon sugar
  salt and pepper to taste
½ cup vegetable oil
2 slices ginger (*see index*)
3 stalks scallion, sliced
1 cup chicken stock

Put chestnuts in boiling water and cook for 20 minutes, then shell and peel. Wash chicken, then cut in pieces and drain. Mix with sherry, soy sauce, sugar, salt, and pepper. Fry in oil until light brown. Add ginger, scallion, and stock. Bring to a boil, reduce heat, and simmer 5 minutes. Add chestnuts and simmer 30 minutes longer. Serve hot.

FRIED MARINATED CHICKEN

Ajam Tjuka Goreng

4 servings

1 2–2½-pound chicken
1 cup water
2 cups vinegar
  salt and pepper to taste
2 cups vegetable oil
1 tablespoon ground hot red pepper*
2 tablespoons lemon juice

Wash chicken and cut in pieces. Put into boiling water and simmer 10 minutes. Add vinegar, salt, and pepper and simmer 10 minutes longer. Drain well. Heat oil and fry chicken until golden brown. Serve with a mixture of red pepper and lemon juice on the side.

Variation: FRIED MARINATED DUCK

Bebek Tjuka Goreng

4 servings

Follow same procedure as in Fried Marinated Chicken, but replace chicken with 1 2½–3-pound duck.

MARINATED CHICKEN

Ajam Tjuka Bumbu

6 servings

1 2½–3-pound chicken
1 tablespoon vegetable oil
5 whole cloves garlic
1 large onion, sliced
1 cup water
2 cups vinegar
2 tablespoons sugar
3 slices ginger (*see index*)
1 tablespoon turmeric*
2 bay leaves
  salt and pepper to taste

Wash chicken, then cut in pieces and drain. Heat oil and fry garlic and onion for 1 minute. Add water, vinegar, chicken, and remaining ingredients. Bring to a boil, reduce heat, and simmer 30 minutes, or until meat is tender. Serve hot or cold, with hot sauce* on the side.

Variation: MARINATED DUCK

    Bebek Tjuka

       6 servings

Follow same procedure as in Marinated Chicken, but replace chicken with 1 2½–3-pound duck.

BRAISED DUCK WITH GREEN PEPPERS
Bebek Masak Lada Muda

       6 servings

       1 2½–3-pound duck
       1 tablespoon vegetable oil
       1 medium onion, chopped
       1 clove garlic, chopped
       2 tablespoons ground nuts
       5 tablespoons ground hot green pepper*
       1 tablespoon ground ginger
         salt and pepper to taste
       1½ cups coconut milk*

Wash duck, then truss. Roast in a 350° oven for 40 minutes. Remove from oven, cool, and cut in pieces. Heat oil and brown onion and garlic. Add nuts, green pepper, ginger, salt, pepper, and coconut milk. Add duck. Bring to a boil, and simmer 20 minutes. Serve.

CHAPTER 11

CHARCOAL-GRILLED MEAT ON SKEWERS Sates

Since the steel skewers are too big for this kind of food, use bamboo skewers, which can be bought in Chinese and Japanese stores. This meat is usually served with peanut-butter sauce or soy sauce, which is described at the end of this chapter.

CHICKEN ON SKEWERS

Sate Ajam

3 servings

3 chicken breasts, boned
15 bamboo skewers
salt and pepper to taste

Slice chicken in ¾-inch cubes. Place 5 pieces of meat on each skewer. Sprinkle with salt and pepper and let stand 15 minutes. Grill over a moderate charcoal fire, about 10 minutes, or until meat is done turning 2 or 3 times. Serve hot, with a sate sauce (*see index*).

Charcoal-Grilled Meat on Skewers (Sates) · 155

Variation 1: LAMB ON SKEWERS

Sate Kambing

3 servings

Follow same procedure as in Chicken on Skewers, but replace chicken with 1½ pounds lean lamb, boned and cut in ¾-inch cubes.

Variation 2: PORK ON SKEWERS

Sate Babi

3 servings

Follow same procedure as in Chicken on Skewers, but replace chicken with 1½ pounds lean pork, boned and cut in ¾-inch cubes.

Variation 3: BEEF ON SKEWERS

Sate Daging

3 servings

Follow same procedure as in Chicken on Skewers, but replace chicken with 1½ pounds sirloin steak, cut in ¾-inch cubes.

BEEF ON SKEWERS WITH SPICES I

Sate Manis

3 servings

1½ pounds sirloin steak
1 teaspoon ground caraway
1 teaspoon ground coriander
1 teaspoon ground garlic
1 tablespoon brown sugar
2 tablespoons soy sauce
1 tablespoon lemon juice
  salt and pepper to taste
15 bamboo skewers

Cut meat in ¾-inch cubes and mix with spices, sugar, garlic, soy sauce, and lemon juice. Marinate 1 hour. Place 5 to 6 pieces of meat on each skewer. Grill over a charcoal fire, turning 2 or 3 times, for about 10 minutes, or until meat is done. Serve hot, with a sate sauce (*see index*).

Variation 1:

CHICKEN ON SKEWERS WITH SPICES I

Sate Ajam Manis

3 servings

Follow same procedure as in Beef on Skewers with Spices I, but replace beef with 3 chicken breasts, boned and cut in ¾-inch cubes.

Variation 2: PORK ON SKEWERS WITH SPICES I

Sate Babi Manis

3 servings

Follow same procedure as in Beef on Skewers with Spices I, but replace beef with 1½ pounds lean pork, boned and cut in ¾-inch cubes.

BEEF ON SKEWERS WITH SPICES II

Sate Bumbu Dendeng

3 servings

1½ pounds sirloin steak
1 tablespoon chopped garlic
1 tablespoon chopped onion
1 tablespoon ground coriander
1 teaspoon ground caraway
½ cup coconut milk*
1 tablespoon soy sauce
   salt and pepper to taste
15 bamboo skewers

Cut beef in ¾-inch cubes and marinate in a mixture of all the other ingredients for 1 hour. Place 5 to 6 pieces of meat on each skewer and grill over charcoal fire, turning 2 or 3 times, 10 minutes, or until meat is done. Serve hot, with a sate sauce (*see index*).

Variation 1:

CHICKEN ON SKEWERS WITH SPICES II

Sate Ajam Bumbu Dendeng

3 servings

Follow same procedure as in Beef on Skewers with Spices II, but replace beef with 3 chicken breasts, boned and cut in ¾-inch cubes.

Variation 2: PORK ON SKEWERS WITH SPICES II

Sate Babi Bumbu Dendeng

3 servings

Follow same procedure as in Beef on Skewers with Spices

II, but replace beef with 1½ pounds lean pork, boned and cut in ¾-inch cubes.

Variation 3: *LAMB ON SKEWERS WITH SPICES II*

Sate Kambing Bumbu Dendeng

3 servings

Follow same procedure as in Beef on Skewers with Spices II, but replace beef with 1½ pounds lean lamb, boned and cut in ¾-inch cubes.

BEEF ON SKEWERS WITH SPICES III

Sate Bumbu Kuning

3 servings

1½ pounds sirloin steak
1 tablespoon chopped onion
1 tablespoon chopped garlic
1 tablespoon ground coriander
1 teaspoon ground caraway
1 tablespoon turmeric*
½ cup grated coconut*
½ cup coconut milk*
1 teaspoon ground ginger
2 tablespoons lemon juice
3 tablespoons brown sugar
salt and pepper to taste
15 bamboo skewers

Cut beef in ¾-inch cubes. Put in a pan, add all other ingredients, and bring to a boil. Cook about 8 minutes, or until meat is just underdone. Place 5 to 6 pieces of meat on each skewer and grill on moderate heat, turning 2 or 3 times, about 8 minutes, or until meat is done. Serve hot, with a sate sauce (*see index*).

Variation 1:

CHICKEN ON SKEWERS WITH SPICES III

Sate Ajam Bumbu Kuning

3 servings

Follow same procedure as in Beef on Skewers with Spices III, but replace beef with 3 chicken breasts, boned and cut in ¾-inch cubes.

Variation 2: PORK ON SKEWERS WITH SPICES III

Sate Babi Bumbu Kuning

3 servings

Follow same procedure as in Beef on Skewers with Spices III, but replace beef with 1½ pounds lean pork, boned and cut in ¾-inch cubes.

Variation 3: LAMB ON SKEWERS WITH SPICES III

Sate Kambing Bumbu Kuning

3 servings

Follow same procedure as in Beef on Skewers with Spices III, but replace beef with 1½ pounds lean lamb, boned and cut in ¾-inch cubes.

CHICKEN ON SKEWERS SURABAJA STYLE[1]

Sate Ajam Surabaja

3 servings

3 chicken breasts, boned
2 tablespoons soy sauce
1 teaspoon chopped garlic
salt and pepper to taste
15 bamboo skewers

Cut chicken in ¾-inch cubes and marinate in a mixture of soy sauce, garlic, salt, and pepper for 1 hour. Place 5 to 6 pieces of meat on each skewer and grill over charcoal fire, turning 2 or 3 times, 10 minutes, or until meat is done. Serve hot, with a sate sauce (*see index*).

Variation 1: BEEF ON SKEWERS SURABAJA STYLE

Sate Surabaja

3 servings

Follow same procedure as in Chicken on Skewers Surabaja Style, but replace chicken with 1½ pounds sirloin steak, cut in ¾-inch cubes.

---

[1] Surabaja is a city on the east coast of Java.

Variation 2: PORK ON SKEWERS SURABAJA STYLE

Sate Babi Surabaja

3 servings

Follow same procedure as in Chicken on Skewers Surabaja Style, but replace chicken with 1½ pounds lean pork, boned and cut in ¾-inch cubes.

Variation 3:

LAMB ON SKEWERS SURABAJA STYLE

Sate Kambing Surabaja

3 servings

Follow same procedure as in Chicken on Skewers Surabaja Style, but replace chicken with 1½ pounds lean lamb, boned and cut in ¾-inch cubes.

BEEF ON SKEWERS PADANG STYLE[1]

Sate Padang

5 servings

½ pound sirloin steak
½ pound beef tripe
½ pound beef liver
½ pound beef heart
1 tablespoon chopped onion

[1] Padang is a city in West Sumatra.

1 tablespoon chopped garlic
2 tablespoons ground hot red pepper*
   salt and pepper to taste
½ cup tamarind juice (*see index*)
1 tablespoon turmeric*
1 cup water
20–25 bamboo skewers

Cut beef, liver, tripe, and heart into ¾-inch cubes. Put in a pan and add remaining ingredients. Bring to a boil, reduce heat, and simmer 40 minutes. Drain, reserving liquid for sauce. Place a mixed selection (5 or 6 pieces) of beef, tripe, liver, and heart on each skewer and grill on low heat, turning 2 or 3 times, about 10 minutes. Place on a serving plate and serve the following sauce over it.

Sauce for Beef on Skewers Padang Style:

½ cup rice flour*
2 cups water
   liquid from Beef on Skewers, above
   salt and pepper to taste

Mix rice flour with water. Add liquid, pepper, and salt. Bring to a boil, reduce heat, and simmer 10 minutes, stirring constantly. If sauce is too thick, add water. This sauce should be served piping hot, poured over the sates.

PORK ON SKEWERS WITH SOY SAUCE

Sate Babi Bumbu Ketjap

3 servings

1½ pounds lean pork, boned
½ cup soy sauce
1 tablespoon chopped onion
1 tablespoon chopped garlic
salt and pepper to taste
15 bamboo skewers

Cut meat in ¾-inch cubes, then wash and drain. Put in a pan, add all other ingredients, and marinate for 1 hour. Remove, place on skewers, and grill on moderate heat until meat is done, about 10 minutes. Serve hot, with a sate sauce (*see index*).

PORK ON SKEWERS PADANG STYLE[1]

Sate Babi Padang

3 servings

1½ pounds lean pork, boned
1 tablespoon chopped onion
1 teaspoon turmeric*
salt and pepper to taste
2 cups coconut milk*
2 tablespoons ground hot red pepper*
15 bamboo skewers

Cut pork in ¾-inch cubes, then wash and drain. Put in a pan and add all other ingredients. Bring to a boil, reduce heat, and simmer 30 minutes. Remove meat, reserve sauce. Place 5 to 6 pieces of meat on each skewer and grill on a moderate fire, turning 2 or 3 times, about 10 minutes. Serve hot, with the sauce poured over it.

[1] Padang is a city in West Sumatra.

SAUCES FOR MEAT ON SKEWERS

Saos Sate

SOY SAUCE WITH BUTTER

Saos Sate Ketjap

½ stick butter (¼ cup)
½ cup soy sauce
2 tablespoons lemon juice
salt and pepper to taste
1 tablespoon ground hot red pepper*
½ cup fried crisp onion flakes (*see index*)

Melt butter in a frying pan and add all ingredients except onion flakes. Bring to a boil, reduce heat, and simmer 2 minutes. Serve the sauce with onion flakes on top.

PEANUT-BUTTER SAUCE

Saos Sate Katjang

1 cup water
3 tablespoons peanut butter
1 tablespoon ground hot red pepper*
salt to taste
2 tablespoons lemon juice
½ cup fried crisp onion flakes (*see index*)

Mix all ingredients, except onion flakes, together. Serve with onion flakes on top.

CHAPTER 12

EGG DISHES
Masakan Telur

OMELET WITH COCONUT MILK

Telur Dadar Bumbu

4 servings

6 medium eggs
2 hot red peppers, sliced*
½ teaspoon shrimp paste*
salt and pepper to taste
1 tablespoon chopped onion
1 teaspoon chopped garlic
1 tablespoon chopped scallion
2 tablespoons coconut milk*
¼ cup vegetable oil

Beat eggs and add all ingredients except oil. Pour mixture into hot oil and fry on both sides until golden brown.

OMELET SUMATRAN STYLE

Telur Gembung

4 servings

6 medium eggs
1 medium onion, chopped
2 hot red peppers, sliced*
salt and pepper to taste
1 tablespoon water
¼ cup vegetable oil

Beat eggs and add all ingredients except oil. Heat oil at high temperature. When oil is very hot, pour in egg mixture and fry both sides golden brown. (Because of the high heat of the oil, the omelet will be very soft and hollow inside.)

STEAMED EGGS

Telur Kukus

4 servings

6 medium eggs
2 tablespoons chopped celery
2 tablespoons chopped Smithfield ham
1 tablespoon chopped onion
1 teaspoon chopped garlic
salt and pepper to taste
1 tablespoon sherry

Beat eggs and add other ingredients. Mix well and pour in a heat-proof dish. Steam 1 hour. Serve hot.

EGGS JAVANESE STYLE

Sambal Goreng Telur

6 servings

6 large eggs, hard-cooked
1 tablespoon vegetable oil
1 medium onion, sliced
2 cloves garlic, sliced
1 teaspoon shrimp paste*
½ cup tamarind juice (*see index*)
  salt to taste
2 tablespoons ground hot red pepper*
1 cup coconut milk*
1 tablespoon brown sugar
1 bay leaf

Shell eggs and make a ½-inch cross on top of each. Heat oil and fry onion and garlic 2 minutes. Add shrimp paste, tamarind juice, salt, red pepper, coconut milk, sugar, bay leaf, and eggs. Bring to a boil, reduce heat, simmer 20 minutes.

HARD-COOKED EGGS
WITH HOT RED PEPPER
Telur Pindang

6 servings

6 large eggs, hard-cooked
1 tablespoon vegetable oil
2 tablespoons ground hot red pepper*
1 teaspoon shrimp paste*
½ cup tamarind juice (*see index*)
1 cup water
½ teaspoon turmeric*
salt to taste

Shell eggs and make a ½-inch cross on top of each. Heat oil and fry red pepper and shrimp paste for 1 minute. Add tamarind juice, water, turmeric, salt, and eggs. Bring to a boil, reduce heat, and simmer 20 minutes. Cut eggs in half, pour sauce over, and serve.

HARD-COOKED EGGS WITH SOY SAUCE
Telur Lo

6 servings

6 large eggs, hard-cooked
½ cup water
2 tablespoons soy sauce
1 tablespoon ground cinnamon
1 tablespoon ground onion
1 teaspoon ground garlic
salt and pepper to taste

Shell eggs. With a fork, prick fine holes on surface of eggs, then cut ½-inch cross on top of each. Mix water with all other ingredients. Put in eggs and bring to a boil. Reduce heat and simmer 30 minutes, or until all sauce has been absorbed. Cut eggs in half and serve with mustard.

FRIED EGGS WITH HOT RED PEPPER
Telur Belada

6 servings

6 large eggs, hard-cooked
½ cup vegetable oil
1 tablespoon chopped onion
2 tablespoons ground hot red pepper*
1 tablespoon lemon juice
   salt to taste

Shell eggs and fry in hot oil, turning several times, until golden brown. Take out eggs and remove all but 1 tablespoon oil. Fry onion and red pepper 2 minutes. Add lemon juice and stir 1 minute. Add eggs and stir 1 minute longer. Cut eggs in half, pour sauce over, and serve.

BRAISED EGGS

Semoor Telur

6 servings

6 large eggs, hard-cooked
½ cup vegetable oil
½ medium onion, sliced
2 tablespoons soy sauce
4 whole cloves
1 cup water
1 teaspoon ground cinnamon

Shell eggs. Heat oil and fry eggs until golden brown. Take out eggs and remove all but 1 tablespoon oil. Add onion and fry 2 minutes. Add soy sauce and remaining ingredients. Make a ½-inch cross on top of each egg and add to mixture. Bring to a boil, reduce heat, and simmer, covered, 30 minutes. Serve.

HARD-COOKED EGGS IN COCONUT MILK

Besengek Telur

6 servings

6 large eggs, hard-cooked
.1 tablespoon vegetable oil
½ medium onion, minced
1 teaspoon turmeric*
1 teaspoon shrimp paste*
1 tablespoon lemon juice
1 tablespoon sugar
1 teaspoon ground caraway
1 tablespoon ground coriander
2 cups coconut milk*

Shell eggs and make a ½-inch cross on top of each. Heat oil and fry onion 2 minutes, then add remaining ingredients and eggs. Bring to a boil, reduce heat, and simmer 20 minutes. Cut eggs in half, pour sauce over, and serve.

EGGS BALINESE STYLE

Telur Masak Bali

6 servings

6 large eggs, hard-cooked
½ cup vegetable oil
½ medium onion, minced
1 clove garlic, minced
1 teaspoon shrimp paste*
1 teaspoon chopped ginger*
1 tablespoon soy sauce
1 cup water
1 tablespoon sugar
1 tablespoon tamarind juice (*see index*)
salt to taste

Shell eggs. Heat oil and fry eggs golden brown. Take out eggs and remove oil, leaving 1 tablespoon in frying pan. Add onion and garlic and fry 2 minutes. Add eggs and remaining ingredients. Bring to a boil, reduce heat, and simmer 20 minutes. When serving, cut eggs in half and pour sauce over.

MARINATED EGGS

Atjar Telur

6 servings

6 large eggs, hard-cooked
½ cup vinegar
3 slices ginger
1 teaspoon turmeric*
1 small onion, sliced
1 tablespoon sugar
2 hot red peppers, cut lengthwise*
1 cup boiling water

Shell eggs. Make a ½-inch cross on top of each egg. Put eggs and remaining ingredients in boiling water. Reduce heat and simmer 10 minutes. Serve hot or cold.

SALTED EGGS

Telur Asin

5 servings

10 duck eggs
water to cover
1 tablespoon whiskey
1 cup salt

Put eggs in water, then add whiskey and salt. Keep eggs four weeks in this salted water. Remove and cook 20 minutes. Serve hot or cold.

CHAPTER 13

VEGETABLES
Masak Sajuran

Most vegetables in Indonesian cooking are stir-fried in such a way that their crispness, color, and taste are preserved. If a very hot pan is used, vegetables usually take no more than 4–10 minutes of cooking. Never overcook vegetables; stop cooking when the color is between bright and dark green. Only in this way will the taste and crispness be maintained.

Cut up the raw vegetables in bite-size pieces and as indicated on p. 238, wash, and drain. Heat a skillet, add oil and onion or garlic, stir 2 or 3 minutes to extract the flavor, and when the skillet is very hot, add vegetables. Sauté over high heat, stirring and mixing.

If the vegetables do not have sufficient juices of their own, a tiny amount of water should be added, the pot covered, and the vegetables allowed to steam 4 or 5 minutes. For vegetables with a strong texture, like green beans, cabbage, and broccoli, more time for cooking is needed.

Leafy vegetables are at their best when served half tender and half crisp.

SAUTÉED TOMATOES

Tumis Tomat

3 *servings*

3 large tomatoes
1 tablespoon vegetable oil
½ medium onion, sliced
salt to taste

Cut tomatoes in wedges. Heat oil and fry onion and salt 2 minutes. Add tomatoes, stir 5 minutes, and serve hot.

SAUTÉED WHITE CABBAGE

Tumis Kol

4 *servings*

2 cups shredded cabbage
1 tablespoon vegetable oil
½ medium onion, sliced
1 tablespoon dried shrimp*
salt to taste
¼ cup water

Heat oil and fry onion, shrimp, and salt, stirring 2 minutes. Add cabbage and stir. Add water, cover pan, and simmer 8 minutes. Serve.

SAUTÉED CAULIFLOWER

Tumis Blum Kol

4 servings

1 large cauliflower, sliced
1 tablespoon vegetable oil
½ medium onion, sliced
1 tablespoon dried shrimp*
salt to taste
¼ cup water

Heat oil and fry onion, shrimp, and salt 2 minutes. Add cauliflower and stir, then add water and simmer 3 minutes. Serve.

SAUTÉED MUSHROOMS

Tumis Djamur

4 servings

1 pound mushrooms, sliced
2 tablespoons vegetable oil
salt to taste
½ medium onion, sliced
1 teaspoon soy sauce
1 tablespoon sherry
1 teaspoon sugar
1 teaspoon cornstarch,
mixed with 2 tablespoons water

Place oil over high heat. Add salt and onion and fry 2 minutes. Add mushrooms, soy sauce, sherry, and sugar and bring to a boil. Reduce heat and simmer 5 minutes. Add cornstarch-water mixture and simmer 3 minutes more. Serve.

SAUTEED CHINESE MUSHROOMS

Tumis Djamur Kering

3 servings

¼ pound Chinese mushrooms*
2 tablespoons vegetable oil
1 clove garlic, sliced
  salt and pepper to taste
1 tablespoon sherry
1 teaspoon sugar
½ teaspoon ground cinnamon
1 cup water

Soak mushrooms 2 hours in water, then drain. Heat oil, add garlic, and stir-fry 1 minute. Add all other ingredients, cover, and simmer 30 minutes.

SAUTEED MUSTARD GREENS

Tumis Sawi Hidjau

4 servings

1 pound mustard greens, sliced
2 tablespoons vegetable oil
½ medium onion, sliced
2 cloves garlic, sliced
  salt and pepper to taste
1 small egg

Wash mustard greens, drain, and cut into 1½-inch lengths. Heat oil and fry onion and garlic 2 minutes. Add greens, salt, and pepper and simmer 10 minutes. Break egg into mixture, stir, and cook 5 minutes longer.

SAUTÉED BEAN SPROUTS

Tumis Tauge

4 servings

1 pound bean sprouts*
1 tablespoon vegetable oil
½ medium onion, sliced
  salt to taste

Wash bean sprouts, then drain. Heat oil and fry onion and salt 2 minutes. Add bean sprouts, stir-fry 3 minutes, remove, and serve.

SAUTÉED GREEN BEANS

Tumis Buntjies

4 servings

1 pound green beans
1 tablespoon vegetable oil
½ medium onion, sliced
1 tablespoon dried shrimp*
  salt to taste
¼ cup water

Remove both ends of beans and cut diagonally in 1-inch slices. Heat oil and fry onion, shrimp, and salt 3 minutes. Add beans, stir, and add water. Cover pan and simmer 10 minutes, or until beans are tender. Serve.

SAUTÉED SNOW PEAS

Tumis Katjang Kapri

4 servings

1 pound snow peas*
1 tablespoon oil
½ medium onion, sliced
salt to taste

Wash snow peas and remove both ends. Heat oil and fry onion with salt 2 minutes. Add snow peas, stir-fry 3 minutes, and serve.

SAUTÉED BAMBOO SHOOTS

Tumis Rebung

4 servings

2 cups bamboo shoots, sliced*
1 tablespoon vegetable oil
½ medium onion, sliced
1 tablespoon dried shrimp*
salt to taste

Heat oil and fry onion, shrimp, and salt 2 minutes. Add bamboo shoots and stir-fry 5 minutes. Serve.

SAUTÉED CHINESE CABBAGE

Tumis Sajur Putih, Petsay

4 servings

    1 pound Chinese cabbage,
       sliced in 1½-inch lengths*
    1 tablespoon vegetable oil
    ½ medium onion, sliced
    1 tablespoon dried shrimp*
       salt to taste

Heat oil and fry onion, shrimp, and salt 2 minutes. Add cabbage and stir, then cover pan and simmer 5–7 minutes. Serve.

SAUTÉED SPINACH

Tumis Bajem

4 servings

    1 pound spinach
    1 tablespoon vegetable oil
    ½ medium onion, sliced
       salt to taste

Wash spinach thoroughly several times in a lot of water, then drain. Heat oil and fry onion and salt 2 minutes. Add spinach, stir, cover pan, and simmer 7 minutes. Serve hot.

SAUTÉED CUCUMBERS

Tumis Ketimun

4 servings

3 medium cucumbers
1 tablespoon vegetable oil
½ medium onion, sliced
1 tablespoon dried shrimp*
salt to taste

Peel cucumbers and cut in rounds ¼ inch thick. Heat oil and fry onion, shrimp, and salt 2 minutes. Add cucumber, stir, cover pan, and simmer 8 minutes. Serve.

SAUTÉED EGGPLANT

Tumis Terong

3 servings

2 medium eggplants
2 tablespoons vegetable oil
½ medium onion, sliced
1 clove garlic, sliced
1 tablespoon dried shrimp*
salt and pepper to taste

Wash eggplants and cut in 1½-inch cubes. Heat oil and fry onion and garlic 2 minutes. Add shrimp and eggplant, stir, and cover pan. Simmer 10 minutes. If there is not sufficient juice, add ¼ cup water. Add salt and pepper and serve hot

EGGPLANT WITH COCONUT MILK

Masak Djeruk Terong

3 servings

2 medium eggplants
1 tablespoon vegetable oil
1 teaspoon shrimp paste*
1 tablespoon ground hot red pepper*
1 cup coconut milk*
   salt to taste

Wash eggplants and cut in 1½-inch cubes. Heat oil, add shrimp paste, and fry 1 minute. Add red pepper and fry 1 minute. Add coconut milk, eggplant, and salt. Bring to a boil and simmer 20 minutes, or until coconut milk is absorbed.

MIXED VEGETABLES I

Sajur Asam Biasa

4 servings

1 small eggplant, cut in 1-inch cubes
1 ear corn, cut in 1-inch slices
½ cup green beans, cut in 1-inch slices
1 small onion, sliced
½ cup peanuts, blanched
½ cup sliced cabbage
2 tablespoons brown sugar
2 bay leaves
2 tablespoons tamarind juice (*see index*)
   salt to taste
2 cups water

Put all ingredients in a pan and bring to a boil. Reduce heat and simmer 20 minutes. Serve with a hot relish.

Vegetables (Masak Sajuran) · *183*

MIXED VEGETABLES II

Sajur Asam Betawi

> *4 servings*
>
>> 1 teaspoon shrimp paste*
>> 1 teaspoon ground red pepper*
>> 2 tablespoons tamarind juice (*see index*)
>> 2 bay leaves
>> 1 small onion, sliced
>> 1 clove garlic, sliced
>> 1 cup sliced cabbage
>> 1 cup green beans, cut in 1-inch slices
>> ½ cup peanuts, blanched
>> salt to taste
>> 2 cups water

Boil water and add all ingredients. Reduce heat and simmer 20 minutes. Serve with the sauce.

MIXED VEGETABLES III

Sajur Menir

> *2 servings*
>
>> 3 ears corn
>> 2 cups water
>> ½ pound spinach
>> 1 small onion, sliced
>> 1 clove garlic, sliced
>> salt to taste

Cut the corn from the cob. Put in boiling water with remaining ingredients. Reduce heat and simmer 20 minutes. Serve with the sauce.

BAMBOO SHOOTS WITH COCONUT MILK I

Sajur Lelawar

3 servings

1 teaspoon shrimp paste*
1 teaspoon tamarind juice (see index)
1 teaspoon ground coriander
1 teaspoon ground caraway
1 clove garlic
1 tablespoon ground hot red pepper*
1 cup water
  salt to taste
2 cups sliced bamboo shoots
1 cup coconut milk*

Put all ingredients except coconut milk into boiling water. Reduce heat and simmer 5 minutes. Add coconut milk and cook, stirring occasionally, 10 minutes.

BAMBOO SHOOTS WITH COCONUT MILK II

Rebung Masak Kelapa

4 servings

2 cups coconut milk*
2 tablespoons ground hot red pepper*
1 teaspoon turmeric*
  salt to taste
5 mint leaves
2 cups sliced bamboo shoots*

Heat coconut milk and add all other ingredients. Bring to a boil, reduce heat, and simmer 20 minutes.

GREEN BEANS WITH COCONUT MILK

Sajur Sambal Buntjies

4 servings

3 cups green beans, cut in 1-inch slices
1 tablespoon shrimp paste*
1 tablespoon vegetable oil
1 tablespoon ground hot red pepper*
  salt to taste
1 cup coconut milk*

Heat oil, add shrimp paste, and fry 1 minute. Add red pepper and stir 2 minutes. Add coconut milk, beans, and salt and bring to a boil. Reduce heat and simmer 20 minutes, or until coconut milk has been partially absorbed.

MIXED VEGETABLES
WITH COCONUT MILK I

Sajur Sambal Godog

6 servings

2 tablespoons vegetable oil
1 tablespoon ground hot red pepper*
½ cup ground dried shrimp*
1 teaspoon turmeric*
  salt to taste
2 bay leaves
1 cup green beans, cut in 1-inch slices
1 cup sliced bamboo shoots*
1 cup Brussels sprouts
1 cup sliced cabbage
2 cups coconut milk*

Heat oil and fry red pepper and shrimp for 2 minutes. Add all other ingredients and bring to a boil. Reduce heat and simmer 20 minutes.

MIXED VEGETABLES
WITH COCONUT MILK II

Sajur Lode

6 servings
1 tablespoon vegetable oil
1 medium onion, sliced
2 cloves garlic, sliced
1 teaspoon shrimp paste*
1 cup sliced green peppers
1 cup green beans, cut in 1-inch slices
1 cup eggplant, cut in 1-inch cubes
1 cup cabbage, cut in 1-inch squares
3 cups coconut milk*
   salt to taste
½ cup water
2 bay leaves
4 small eggs, hard-cooked

Heat oil and fry onion, garlic, and shrimp paste 2 minutes. Add all the vegetables, salt, and water. Bring to a boil, reduce heat, and simmer 10 minutes. Shell eggs, make a ½-inch cross on top of each, and add to mixture. Add bay leaves and coconut milk and simmer 10 minutes longer.

MIXED VEGETABLES
WITH CURRY SAUCE

Sajur Kerie

6 servings

1 tablespoon oil
½ medium onion, minced
3 cloves garlic, minced
1 tablespoon curry powder*
1 tablespoon ground coriander
1 teaspoon ground caraway
½ cup water
1 cup sliced green peppers
1 cup cabbage, cut in 1-inch squares
1 cup green beans, cut in 1-inch slices
1 cup cucumbers, cut in 1-inch squares
½ cup shining noodles*
2 bay leaves
salt to taste
2 cups coconut milk*

Heat oil and fry onion and garlic 2 minutes. Add curry powder, other spices, water, vegetables, shining noodles, and bay leaves. Bring to a boil, reduce heat, and simmer 10 minutes. Add coconut milk and salt. Simmer 10 minutes longer, or until vegetables are tender.

MIXED VEGETABLES
WITH CHICKEN STOCK

Gulai Tjampur-Tjampur, Sajur Kim Lo

4 servings

2 cups chicken stock
½ cup shining noodles*

½ cup cloud ears*
½ cup tiger lilies*
½ cup peanuts, blanched
1 cup cabbage, cut in 1-inch squares
1 cup green beans, cut in 1-inch slices
1 cup cucumber, cut in 1-inch squares
½ cup fried crisp onion flakes (see index)

Soak shining noodles, cloud ears and tiger lilies 10 minutes in water. Drain. Cut tiger lilies in ½-inch pieces. Remove hard stem. Heat stock and add all ingredients except onion flakes. Bring to a boil, reduce heat, and simmer 20 minutes. Serve hot, with onion flakes on top.

TOMATOES WITH COCONUT MILK

Sajur Tomat

4 servings

6 medium tomatoes, cut in wedges
1 tablespoon vegetable oil
1 small onion, sliced
1 clove garlic, sliced
2 tablespoons ground hot red pepper*
1 teaspoon shrimp paste*
1 cup coconut milk*
1 bay leaf
  salt to taste
1 tablespoon sugar

Heat oil and fry onion, garlic, red pepper, and shrimp paste 2 minutes. Add coconut milk, bay leaf, salt, and sugar. Bring to a boil, reduce heat, and simmer 15 minutes, or until mixture has been reduced to ½ cup. Add tomato wedges and stir 3 minutes. Serve.

MIXED VEGETABLES JAVANESE STYLE I

Sajur Ketewel

4 servings

2 cups coconut milk*
2 cups cabbage, cut in 1-inch squares
1 small onion, sliced
2 cloves garlic, sliced
2 bay leaves
1 tablespoon ground coriander
1 teaspoon ground caraway
1 tablespoon ground hot red pepper*
2 tablespoons ground nuts
1 teaspoon shrimp paste*
2 bean cakes, cut in 1-inch squares*
4 small eggs, hard-cooked

Heat coconut milk and add all ingredients except bean cakes and eggs. Bring to a boil, reduce heat, and simmer 10 minutes. Shell eggs and make a ½-inch cross on top of each. Add eggs and bean cakes to mixture and simmer 10 minutes longer. Serve.

MIXED VEGETABLES JAVANESE STYLE II

Sajur Gudeg

4 servings

2 cups coconut milk*
2 cups cabbage, cut in 1-inch squares
1 small onion, sliced
2 cloves garlic, sliced
   salt to taste
2 bay leaves
1 tablespoon ground coriander
1 teaspoon ground caraway
2 tablespoons sugar
4 bean cakes, cut in 1-inch cubes*

Bring coconut milk to a boil. Add all other ingredients, reduce heat, and simmer 20 minutes, or until vegetables are tender.

MIXED VEGETABLES
WITH PEANUT SAUCE I
Petjel

6 servings

3 tablespoons peanut butter
salt to taste
1½ cups water
1 teaspoon shrimp paste°
1 clove garlic, minced
1 tablespoon brown sugar
1 tablespoon ground hot red pepper°
1 tablespoon lemon juice
1 cup sliced cabbage
1 cup diced green beans
1 pound spinach
1 cup bean sprouts°

Make a thick sauce by mixing peanut butter, salt, water, shrimp paste, garlic, sugar, red pepper, and lemon juice. Bring to a boil, reduce heat, and simmer 2 minutes. Cool.

Boil cabbage and beans in water to cover 20 minutes. Add spinach and simmer 5 minutes longer. Add bean sprouts and stir 1 minute, then drain. Put vegetables on a large serving plate, pour sauce over, and serve immediately.

MIXED VEGETABLES
WITH PEANUT SAUCE II
Gado-Gado

6 servings

½ cup peanut butter
1 clove garlic, minced
1 tablespoon brown sugar
1 cup coconut milk*
1 tablespoon lemon juice
salt to taste
1 cup sliced cabbage
1 cup sliced carrots
1 cup green beans, cut in 1-inch slices
1 pound spinach
1 cup bean sprouts*
2 medium potatoes, boiled and sliced
2 large eggs, hard-cooked
1 medium cucumber, sliced
½ cup fried crisp onion flakes (see index)
2 cups shrimp puffs (see index)

Make a sauce by mixing peanut butter, garlic, sugar, coconut milk, lemon juice, and salt. Bring to a boil, reduce heat, and simmer 2 minutes. Add water if the sauce is too thick.

Boil cabbage, carrots, green beans, and spinach in water 20 minutes. One minute before other vegetables are done, add bean sprouts, stir, and drain. Place vegetables on a large serving plate and garnish with sliced potatoes, sliced eggs, sliced cucumber, onion flakes, and shrimp puffs. Serve with peanut sauce on the side.

MIXED VEGETABLES WITH COCONUT

Urapan

4 servings

¼ cup water
½ cup grated coconut*
1 small onion, chopped
2 cloves garlic, chopped
2 tablespoons ground hot red pepper*
1 teaspoon shrimp paste*
  salt to taste
1 tablespoon lemon juice
1 cup green beans
1 pound spinach
1 cup bean sprouts*

Mix water with coconut, onion, garlic, red pepper, shrimp paste, salt, and lemon juice. Bring to a boil, reduce heat, and simmer 10 minutes. Boil beans in water 10 minutes. Add spinach and simmer 10 minutes longer, then add bean sprouts, mix, and drain. Add vegetables to coconut mixture and serve.

BEAN SPROUT DISH

Gado-Gado Penganten

4 servings

1 tablespoon vegetable oil
2 tablespoons ground nuts
1 teaspoon shrimp paste*
2 tablespoons chopped onion
1 cup coconut milk*
  salt to taste
2 tablespoons sugar
1 tablespoon lemon juice
3 cups bean sprouts
½ cup fried crisp onion flakes (*see index*)

Heat oil and fry nuts, shrimp paste, and onion 3 minutes. Add coconut milk, salt, sugar, and lemon juice. Stir 3 minutes, remove, and cool. Pour boiling water over bean sprouts and drain. Pour coconut milk mixture over bean sprouts, garnish with onion flakes, and serve.

CHAPTER 14

SAMBAL
GORENG

VEGETABLE SAMBAL GORENG:
Sambal Goreng Sajur

GREEN BEAN SAMBAL GORENG
Sambal Goreng Buntjies

4 servings

1 tablespoon vegetable oil
1 medium onion, sliced
2 cloves garlic, sliced
1 tablespoon hot red pepper, diagonally sliced*
1 teaspoon shrimp paste*
1 cup coconut milk*
1 tablespoon sugar
2 bay leaves
   salt to taste
2 cups green beans, cut in 1-inch slices
1 tablespoon tamarind juice (*see index*)

Heat oil and fry onion, garlic, red pepper, and shrimp paste 2 minutes. Add coconut milk, sugar, bay leaves, and salt. Bring to a boil, reduce heat, and simmer 5 minutes. Add beans and simmer 20 minutes. Two minutes before serving, add tamarind juice.

Variation 1:

MIXED VEGETABLE SAMBAL GORENG

Sambal Goreng Sajur Majur

6 servings

Follow same procedure as in Green Bean Sambal Goreng, but add 1 cup shredded cabbage, 1 cup Brussels sprouts, 1 cup squash, cut in 1-inch cubes; and 1 cup more of coconut milk* to the beans.

Variation 2: TOMATO SAMBAL GORENG

Sambal Goreng Tomat

4 servings

Follow same procedure as in Green Bean Sambal Goreng, but replace beans with 6 large tomatoes, cut in wedges. Simmer tomatoes only 5 minutes in sauce mixture.

Variation 3: BEAN CAKE SAMBAL GORENG

Sambal Goreng Tahu

4 servings

Follow same procedure as in Green Bean Sambal Goreng, but replace green beans with 4 bean cakes,* cut in 1-inch cubes.

Variation 4:

SALTED SOYBEANS SAMBAL GORENG

Sambal Goreng Taotjo

4 servings

Follow same procedure as in Green Bean Sambal Goreng, but replace green beans with ½ cup salted soybeans* and 2 cups sliced green peppers.

MEAT SAMBAL GORENG:
Sambal Goreng Daging

CHICKEN LIVER SAMBAL GORENG
Sambal Goreng Hati Ajam

6 servings

1 cup gizzards, sliced
1 cup chicken hearts
1 cup sliced chicken livers
6 large eggs, hard-cooked and shelled
1 tablespoon vegetable oil
1 medium onion, sliced
2 cloves garlic, sliced
1 teaspoon shrimp paste*
½ cup hot red peppers, diagonally sliced*
1½ cups coconut milk*
1 tablespoon sugar
2 bay leaves
salt to taste
2 tablespoons tamarind juice (*see index*)

Wash gizzards, hearts, and livers, then drain. Make a ½-inch cross on top of each egg. Heat oil and fry onion, garlic, red pepper, and shrimp paste 2 minutes. Add coconut milk, sugar, bay leaves and salt. Bring to a boil, reduce heat, and simmer 5 minutes. Add gizzards, hearts, and livers and simmer 30 minutes longer. Five minutes before serving, add eggs and tamarind juice.

SHRIMP SAMBAL GORENG

Sambal Goreng Udang

4 servings

1 pound medium shrimp
1 tablespoon vegetable oil
1 medium onion, sliced
2 cloves garlic, sliced
1 teaspoon shrimp paste*
1 tablespoon hot red pepper, diagonally sliced*
1 cup coconut milk*
2 bay leaves
½ tablespoon sugar
  salt to taste
1 tablespoon tamarind juice (*see index*)

Shell shrimp, then clean, split in half, and drain. Heat oil and fry onion, garlic, red pepper, and shrimp paste 2 minutes. Add coconut milk, bay leaves, sugar, and salt. Bring to a boil, reduce heat, and simmer 1 minute. Add shrimp and simmer 10 minutes longer. Two minutes before serving, add tamarind juice.

CRISP SAMBAL GORENG:

Sambal Goreng Krípík

POTATO CHIP SAMBAL GORENG

Sambal Goreng Kripik Kentang

4 servings

2 cups small potato chips
1 tablespoon vegetable oil
1 teaspoon shrimp paste*
2 tablespoons hot red pepper, diagonally sliced*

1 tablespoon tamarind juice (*see index*)
2 tablespoons sugar
½ cup fried crisp onion flakes (*see index*)

Heat oil and fry shrimp paste and red pepper for 5 minutes. Add sugar and tamarind juice and stir 8 minutes, or until mixture is completely dry. Add potato chips and onion flakes and mix carefully. Put in a jar and cover tightly in order to maintain crispness.

DRIED SHRIMP SAMBAL GORENG

Sambal Goreng Ebbie

6 servings

2 tablespoons vegetable oil
1 tablespoon ground hot red pepper
1 tablespoon shrimp paste*
1 cup ground dried shrimp*
1 cup fried crisp onion flakes (*see index*)

Heat oil and fry red pepper and shrimp paste 5–8 minutes, or until mixture is light brown. Add dried shrimp and stir 10 minutes, or until shrimp is crisp. Remove from heat. Add onion flakes and mix. Put in a jar and cover tightly in order to maintain crispness.

Variation 1: CASHEW SAMBAL GORENG

Sambal Goreng Bidji Djambu Monjet

6 servings

Follow same procedure as in Dried Shrimp Sambal Goreng, but add 1 cup fried cashews.

Variation 2: SOYBEAN SAMBAL GORENG

Sambal Goreng Katjang Kedele

6 servings

Follow same procedure as in Dried Shrimp Sambal Goreng, but add 1 cup fried soybeans (*see index*).

POTATO CHIPS WITH RED PEPPER

Sambal Ubi Kentang

4 servings

¼ pound small potato chips
2 tablespoons vegetable oil
1 teaspoon shrimp paste*
3 tablespoons ground hot red pepper*
1 tablespoon lemon juice
salt to taste

Heat oil and fry shrimp paste, red pepper, and lemon juice 5–8 minutes, or until red pepper is light brown. Add chips and mix carefully. Put in a jar and cover tightly in order to maintain crispness.

GRATED COCONUT WITH PEANUT

Serundeng

6 servings

1 tablespoon vegetable oil
1 small onion, chopped
4 cloves garlic, chopped
1 teaspoon shrimp paste*
1 tablespoon ground coriander
1 teaspoon ground caraway
  salt to taste
4 tablespoons brown sugar
1 tablespoon tamarind juice (*see index*)
1 cup grated coconut*
2 cups blanched peanuts, fried

Heat oil and fry onion, garlic and shrimp paste 2 minutes. Add coriander, caraway, salt, sugar, tamarind juice, and coconut. Mix together and fry on low heat, stirring constantly, about 20 minutes, or until mixture is light brown. Add peanuts and mix all together. Put in jar and cover tightly in order to maintain crispness.

GRATED COCONUT WITH DRIED SHRIMP

Bubuk Buras

6 servings

1 tablespoon vegetable oil
2 tablespoons ground nuts
1 tablespoon ground hot red pepper*
1 small onion, chopped
1 teaspoon shrimp paste*
2 tablespoons brown sugar
1 cup grated coconut*
½ cup ground dried shrimp*

Heat oil and fry nuts, red pepper, onion, and shrimp paste 2 minutes. Add sugar, coconut, and shrimp. Over low heat, stir constantly 20 minutes, or until coconut is light brown. This relish is usually served with Rice Cooked with Coconut Milk (Buras) (*see index*). Put in jar and cover tightly in order to maintain crispness.

CHAPTER 15

INDONESIAN RELISHES

Indonesian relishes are divided into three groups:

1 Hot relishes: Sambalans
This group of relishes consists for the most part of ground hot red peppers mixed with different spices, fish, shrimp, or nuts.

2 Sweet relishes: Chutneys or Petjilis
This group consists of vegetables or fruits cooked with sugar and spices.

3 Sweet-and-Sour or Pickled Relishes: Atjars
This group consists of pickled vegetables of different varieties.

HOT RELISHES: Sambalans

HOT SHRIMP PASTE RELISH
Sambal Terasi

8 servings

2 tablespoons shrimp paste*
1 small onion, chopped
½ cup ground hot red peppers*
2 tablespoons lemon juice
salt to taste

Wrap shrimp paste in aluminum foil and bake in moderate (350°) oven 20 minutes, or until light brown. Remove shrimp paste from the oven, chop, and add to remaining ingredients. Mix and serve.

HOT RELISH WITH NUTS
Sambal Badjak

8 servings

½ cup ground hot red peppers*
1 tablespoon shrimp paste*
1 medium onion, chopped
4 cloves garlic, chopped
½ cup chopped nuts
salt to taste
½ cup water
1 tablespoon brown sugar
3 tablespoons vegetable oil

Mix red pepper with all other ingredients. Stirring constantly, fry mixture 20 minutes, or until all liquid has been absorbed.

HOT COCONUT RELISH

Sambal Kelapa

8 servings

1 cup grated coconut*
½ cup ground hot red peppers
1 tablespoon shrimp paste*
1 medium onion, chopped
1 tablespoon sugar
3 cloves garlic, chopped
   salt to taste

Mix all ingredients. Stirring constantly, fry mixture 20 minutes, or until brown and dry.

HOT SOYBEAN RELISH

Sambal Bubuk Kedele

8 servings

1 cup ground fried soybeans (*see index*)
1 medium onion, chopped
½ cup ground hot red peppers*
   salt to taste
2 tablespoons lemon juice
2 cloves garlic, chopped

Mix all ingredients together.

HOT FISH RELISH

Sambal Lingkung

8 servings

½ pound fish fillet
1 cup coconut milk*
½ cup ground hot red peppers*
1 tablespoon shrimp paste*
1 medium onion, chopped
5 cloves garlic, chopped
½ cup chopped nuts
1 tablespoon sugar

Steam fish 30 minutes. Put through the meat grinder, then mix with all other ingredients. Heat frying pan and add mixture. Stirring constantly, fry about 40 minutes, or until mixture is light brown, dry, and crisp. Keep this relish in a tightly covered jar.

HOT SHRIMP RELISH

Sambal Udang

8 servings

2 cups ground dried shrimp*
1 medium onion, chopped
½ cup ground hot red pepper*
1 cup vegetable oil
salt to taste
2 tablespoons lemon juice

Mix all ingredients. Stirring constantly, fry 20 minutes, or until mixture is brown and dry. Keep this relish in a tightly covered jar.

HOT PEANUT RELISH

Sambal Bubuk Katjang

8 servings

2 cups ground fried peanuts
1 tablespoon ground roasted shrimp paste
(*see index*)
½ cup ground hot red peppers*
1 tablespoon sugar
salt to taste

Mix peanuts with all other ingredients.

HOT DRIED FISH RELISH

Sambal Uap

8 servings

1 cup small dried fish*
½ cup ground hot red peppers*
2 tablespoons lemon juice
salt to taste
1 teaspoon cornstarch,
dissolved in 2 tablespoons water
1 medium onion, chopped

Mix dried fish with all other ingredients. Put in a heat-proof bowl and steam 30 minutes.

HOT GREEN PEPPER RELISH

Sambal Petis Bumbu

8 servings

1 tablespoon vegetable oil
1 cup hot green peppers, diagonally sliced*
1 medium onion, sliced
3 cloves garlic, sliced
1 tablespoon sugar
2 tablespoons lemon juice
   salt to taste
1 tablespoon shrimp sauce*

Heat oil and fry green peppers, onion, and garlic 3 minutes. Add remaining ingredients and stir 5 minutes longer on low heat.

HOT FRIED FISH RELISH I

Sambal Ikan Kering Goreng

8 servings

¼ pound any salted dried fish*
½ cup vegetable oil
½ cup ground hot red peppers*
1 medium onion, chopped
2 tablespoons lemon juice
   salt to taste

Wash fish, then drain. Heat oil and fry fish 5 minutes, or until fish is light brown. Remove bones and grind fish. Mix with all other ingredients and fry, stirring constantly, for 10 minutes, or until brown and dry. Put in a tightly covered jar.

HOT FRIED FISH RELISH II
Sambal Ikan Kering

> 8 servings
>
> ¼ pound any salted dried fish *
> ½ cup vegetable oil
> ½ cup ground hot red peppers *
> 1 medium onion, chopped
> 3 tablespoons lemon juice
>   salt to taste

Wash fish, then drain. Heat oil and fry fish 5 minutes, or until fish is light brown. Remove bones and grind fish. Mix with all other ingredients.

SWEET RELISHES: Petjilis

SWEET PINEAPPLE RELISH
Petjili Nanas

> 6 servings
>
> 1 whole pineapple, cut in wedges,
>   or 1 14-ounce can pineapple chunks, drained
> 1 tablespoon vegetable oil
> 1 small onion, sliced
> 2 hot red peppers, diagonally sliced *
> 1 teaspoon ground cinnamon
> 3 tablespoons sugar or ½ cup pineapple juice
>   salt to taste

Heat oil and fry onion and red pepper 2 minutes. Add all other ingredients and cook 10 minutes.

Variation: SWEET MANGO RELISH

> *Petjili Mangga*

>> *4 servings*

Follow same procedure as in Sweet Pineapple Relish, but replace pineapple with 2 cups ripe or young mangoes, cut into 1-inch cubes.

SWEET-AND-SOUR RELISHES: Atjars

SWEET-AND-SOUR RADISH RELISH

Atjar Radys

>> *4 servings*

>> 2 bunches radishes
>> salt to taste
>> ½ cup vinegar
>> 3 tablespoons sugar
>> ¼ cup water

Wash radishes, then cut in half and mix with salt. Let stand 20 minutes, then drain. Heat vinegar. Add sugar, water, and salt and boil 2 minutes. Remove from heat. When cooled, add radishes. Let stand for a few hours before serving.

Variation 1:

> SWEET-AND-SOUR WHITE RADISH RELISH

> *Atjar Lobak*

>> *4 servings*

Follow same procedure as in Sweet-and-Sour Radish Relish, but replace red radishes with 2 cups white radishes, cut in 1-inch cubes.

Variation 2:

SWEET-AND-SOUR CUCUMBER RELISH

Atjar Ketimun

4 servings

Follow same procedure as in Sweet-and-Sour Radish Relish, but replace radishes with 2 medium cucumbers, cut in 1½-inch cubes.

Variation 3:

SWEET-AND-SOUR BAMBOO-SHOOT RELISH

Atjar Rebung

4 servings

Follow same procedure as in Sweet-and-Sour Radish Relish, but replace radishes with 1 cup sliced bamboo shoots.

PICKLED RELISHES: Atjars

PICKLED MIXED VEGETABLE RELISH
Atjar Tjampur Mentah

8 servings

1 cup carrots, sliced julienne
1 cup shredded cabbage
1 cup bean sprouts*
1 tablespoon salt
2 cups vinegar
1 large onion, sliced
5 cloves garlic, whole
  salt to taste
3 tablespoons sugar
2 hot red peppers, split*

Mix vegetables with 1 tablespoon salt. Let stand 20 minutes, then drain. Heat vinegar and add onion, garlic, salt, and sugar. Bring to a boil, reduce heat, and simmer 5 minutes. Remove from heat and cool. Add vegetables and red peppers. Keep overnight before serving.

Variation 1:

PICKLED MIXED VEGETABLE RELISH
WITH TURMERIC
Atjar Tjampur Kuning

8 servings

Ingredients as in Pickled Mixed Vegetable Relish, with the following added:

2 tablespoons turmeric*
¼ cup ground nuts
1 tablespoon chopped garlic
1 tablespoon vegetable oil

Heat oil and fry turmeric, nuts, and garlic 3 minutes. Follow same procedure as in Pickled Mixed Vegetable Relish, and add to vinegar mixture the fried turmeric, garlic, and nuts.

Variation 2:

PICKLED MIXED VEGETABLE RELISH
WITH MUSTARD

Atjar Tjampur Mustard

8 servings

Follow same procedure as in Pickled Mixed Vegetable Relish, but add 3 tablespoons French mustard to the vinegar mixture.

 # FRITTERS

There are three kinds of fritters:

1 *Soft fritters* are made from flour, mashed potatoes, or corn, mixed with vegetables, fish, shrimp, or meat, and deep fried in oil.

2 *Crisp fritters* are prepared from flour, rice flour, or tapioca flour, mixed with vegetables, beans, fish, or shrimp, and deep fried in oil.

3 *Fruit fritters* are prepared from fruit dipped in flour batter and deep fried in oil.

SOFT FRITTERS: Perkedel

POTATO BALLS WITH SHRIMP
Perkedel Udang

6 servings

1 cup shrimp, cooked, shelled, and chopped
1 small onion, chopped
2 cloves garlic, chopped
2 cups mashed potatoes
1 tablespoon cornstarch
2 tablespoons chopped celery
   salt and pepper to taste
2 medium eggs, separated
3 cups vegetable oil

Mix shrimp, onion, and garlic. Mix with potatoes and add cornstarch, celery, salt, pepper, and egg yolks. Mix thoroughly. Beat egg whites. Shape balls the size of a small egg from potato mixture, dip in egg white, and deep fry until light brown. Drain on absorbent paper.

Variation 1: POTATO BALLS WITH BEEF

Perkedel Daging

6 servings

Follow same procedure as in Potato Balls with Shrimp, but replace shrimp with 1 cup chopped beef.

Variation 2: POTATO BALLS WITH PORK

Perkedel Babi

6 servings

Follow same procedure as in Potato Balls with Shrimp, but replace shrimp with 1 cup ground pork.

Variation 3: POTATO BALLS WITH CHICKEN

Perkedel Ajam

6 servings

Follow same procedure as in Potato Balls with Shrimp, but replace shrimp with 1 cup ground chicken.

Variation 4: POTATO BALLS WITH FISH

Perkedel Ikan

6 servings

Follow same procedure as in Potato Balls with Shrimp, but replace shrimp with 1 cup chopped fish.

CORN FRITTERS WITH SHRIMP

Perkedel Djagung

6 servings

6 ears of corn
2 large eggs, beaten
1 tablespoon chopped celery
1 tablespoon chopped garlic
1 cup shrimp, cooked, shelled, and chopped
  salt and pepper to taste
3 cups vegetable oil

Grate corn from ears. Add eggs and all other ingredients except oil. Heat oil. Drop corn mixture into oil, a tablespoonful at a time. Fry until golden brown and drain on absorbent paper.

BEAN CAKE FRITTERS WITH SHRIMP
Perkedel Tahu

6 servings

4 bean cakes, chopped*
1 cup shrimp, cooked, shelled, and chopped
1 tablespoon chopped onion
1 tablespoon chopped garlic
  salt and pepper to taste
1 tablespoon chopped celery
1 tablespoon flour
2 large eggs, beaten
3 cups vegetable oil

Mix bean cakes with all other ingredients except oil. Heat oil. Drop bean cake mixture into oil, a tablespoonful at a time. Fry until golden brown. Drain on absorbent paper.

COCONUT FRITTERS
Rempah

6 servings

2 cups grated coconut*
1 tablespoon chopped onion
1 tablespoon chopped garlic
2 large eggs, beaten
2 tablespoons flour
½ cup coconut milk*
1 tablespoon ground coriander
1 teaspoon ground caraway
  salt and pepper to taste
3 cups vegetable oil

Mix grated coconut with all other ingredients except oil. Heat oil. Drop coconut mixture into hot oil, a tablespoonful at a time. Fry until golden brown. Drain on absorbent paper.

CRISP FRITTERS: Krípík

CRISP PEANUT FRITTERS

Rempejek Katjang Tanah, Kasreng

6 servings

1 cup flour or rice flour*
1 tablespoon ground coriander
1 teaspoon ground caraway
  salt and pepper to taste
1 large egg, beaten
1 tablespoon chopped onion
1 tablespoon chopped garlic
¾ cup coconut milk*
1 teaspoon baking powder
½ cup raw peanuts
3 cups vegetable oil

Mix all ingredients except oil, making a thin batter. Add a bit of water if necessary. Heat oil. Drop large thin fritters into oil and fry until golden brown, turning several times. Drain on absorbent paper.

Variation 1: CRISP SOYBEAN FRITTERS

Rempejek Kedele

6 servings

Follow same procedure as in Crisp Peanut Fritters, but replace peanuts with ½ cup soybeans.*

Variation 2: *CRISP DRIED SHRIMP FRITTERS*

Rempejek Udang

6 servings

Follow same procedure as in Crisp Peanut Fritters, but replace peanuts with ½ cup dried shrimp.°

Variation 3: *CRISP DRIED FISH FRITTERS*

Rempejek Ikan Teri

6 servings

Follow same procedure as in Crisp Peanut Fritters, but replace peanuts with ½ cup small dried fish.°

Variation 4: *CRISP FRESH SHRIMP FRITTERS*

Gimbal Udang, Raki Udang

6 servings

Follow same procedure as in Crisp Peanut Fritters, but replace peanuts with ½ pound fresh medium-size shrimp, shelled or unshelled.

SHRIMP PUFFS

Krupuk

Shrimp puffs (shrimp chips, shrimp wafers) are made in Indonesia from tapioca flour that is mixed with fish, shrimp, and spices, then steamed, cut in thin slices of different sizes, and dried. The shrimp puffs made in Sidoardjo* are well known among foreigners who have been in Indonesia for a long time.

Locally made shrimp puffs can be bought in Chinese grocery stores. These are not made according to the original Indonesian recipe, but the authentic ones can be bought in America (see entry for Mrs. De Wildt, p. 26).

FRIED SHRIMP PUFFS

Krupuk Udang Goreng

4 servings

2 cups vegetable oil
¼ pound shrimp puffs

Heat oil. Drop puffs in, two at a time, and permit them to puff up several times their original size. Turn and drain on absorbent paper. It takes only 1 or 2 minutes for the puffs to expand.

---

* Sidoardjo is a town on the east coast of Java.

FRUIT FRITTERS: Buah-Buahan Goreng

BANANA FRITTERS

Pisang Goreng

6 servings

4 bananas
1 cup flour
⅔ cup water
1 teaspoon baking powder
salt and sugar to taste
3 cups vegetable oil

Peel bananas. Cut diagonally in ¾-inch slices. Mix flour with all other ingredients except oil, making a light batter. Heat oil. Dip bananas in batter and deep fry until golden brown. Drain on absorbent paper.

Variation: PINEAPPLE FRITTERS

Nanas Goreng

4 servings

Follow same procedure as in Banana Fritters, but replace bananas with 1 cup fresh or canned pineapple wedges.

CHAPTER 17

BEVERAGES
Minuman

The Indonesian people in general do not drink alcohol. The most popular drinks are the home-made syrups of different varieties. Because of the hot climate, the long drinks are served cold.

PINEAPPLE SYRUP

Setrup Nanas

8 servings

2 cups sugar
2 cups water
1 cup grated pineapple

Put all ingredients into a pan. Bring to a boil, reduce heat, and simmer 40 minutes. Pour mixture through a sieve. Cool resulting syrup and pour into a bottle. When serving, pour 1½–2 tablespoons in a glass and add crushed ice and water.

Variation 1: GINGER SYRUP

Setrup Djahe

8 servings

Follow same procedure as in Pineapple Syrup, but replace pineapple with 10 slices ginger (*see index*).

Variation 2: TAMARIND SYRUP

Setrup Asem

8 servings

Follow same procedure as in Pineapple Syrup, but replace pineapple with ½ cup tamarind juice (*see index*).

GINGER DRINK

Bandrek

4 servings

4 cups water
1 cup brown sugar
6 slices ginger (*see index*)

Cook all ingredients for 40 minutes on low heat. Pour in cups and serve hot.

This is the most popular drink in Indonesia and usually served hot, especially in the mountain regions.

 *TEA DELICACIES*

FRIED WONTON

Pangsit Goreng

6 servings

40 wonton skins*
1½ cups ground pork
2 tablespoons chopped parsley
1 tablespoon soy sauce
½ cup ground dried shrimp*
1 tablespoon chopped onion
salt and pepper to taste
3 cups vegetable oil

Mix pork with all other ingredients except oil. Place 1 teaspoon of this mixture at the corner of a skin (skins are squares). Fold this corner toward opposite corner. Moisten the other two ends with salt water and seal them together. Heat oil and deep fry wonton until light brown. Drain on absorbent paper.

FRIED EGG ROLL

Lumpia Goreng

6 servings

1 cup sifted flour
2 large eggs, beaten
1 cup water
1 teaspoon salt
3 cups vegetable oil
2 bean cakes, cut julienne*
1 medium onion, sliced
1 clove garlic, sliced
½ cup sliced pork or chicken
½ cup shrimp, cooked, shelled,
    and split lengthwise
2 tablespoons soy sauce
    salt and pepper to taste
1 cup bean sprouts*
½ cup sliced cabbage
½ cup sliced bamboo shoots*

Note: Egg roll wrappers can be bought. See entry, Chapter 2.

Prepare a batter by mixing flour, eggs, water, and salt. Fry thin pancakes, about 8 inches in diameter. Make about 6–8 pancakes.

For the filling, heat about ½ cup of the oil. Fry bean cakes until light brown. Drain. Remove most of oil, leaving 1 table-spoon in frying pan. Fry onion and garlic 2 minutes. Add pork, shrimp, and all other ingredients. Cook 15 minutes. Cool.

Fill each pancake with 2 tablespoons of this mixture. Spread filling out lengthwise and fold pancake envelope fashion (first fold over flap along length of filling, then fold over two flaps along ends of filling; moisten edge of last flap with salt water and seal filling up). Fry the egg rolls in hot oil until golden brown and drain on absorbent paper.

FRIED SHRIMP WITH VEGETABLES

Hepia

6 servings

3 bean cakes, cut julienne*
3 cups vegetable oil
1 medium onion, sliced
½ cup sliced pork or chicken
1 tablespoon soy sauce
 salt and pepper to taste
1½ cup flour
½ cup bean sprouts*
½ cup Chinese leek, cut in 1-inch slices*
12 large shrimps in shell

Fry bean cakes in 2 tablespoons of the oil until light brown. Drain. Fry onion in 1 tablespoon oil for 1 minute, then add pork, bean cakes, soy sauce, salt, and pepper. Cook for 5 minutes. Remove from heat and cool. Gradually add flour to this mixture, stirring well. Add bean sprouts and leek. Mix carefully, and into each 2 tablespoons of the mixture press 1 shrimp. Drop into hot oil and deep fry until light brown. Drain on absorbent paper. Serve with hot sauce* or peanut sauce (*see index*).

STUFFED GLUTINOUS RICE

Lemper Ajam

8 *servings*

1 cup glutinous rice*
1½ cups coconut milk*
    salt and pepper to taste
1 medium onion, sliced
2 cloves garlic, sliced
2 tablespoons butter
1 cup shredded chicken
¼ cup water

Soak rice overnight in water. Drain. Add coconut milk and salt and cook on low heat 20 minutes, or until rice is well done.

Prepare filling as follows: Brown onion and garlic in butter. Add chicken, water, salt, and pepper. Cook on low heat 10 minutes. Cool. Make 8–10 balls of rice. Stuff each with 1 tablespoon of the chicken mixture. Wrap in aluminum foil and heat in moderate (350°) oven for 15 minutes.

RICE COOKED WITH COCONUT MILK

Buras

6 *servings*

2 cups rice
3 cups coconut milk*
    salt to taste

Add rice and salt to coconut milk, bring to a boil, and cook 10 minutes, or until all the coconut milk has been absorbed.

Usually this rice is then cooked in banana leaves. Where banana leaves can not be obtained, replace with a cheese cloth bag, 5 inches long and 1½ inches wide. Put the rice in this bag, sew up, and cook in boiling water for 1½ hours. Remove rice from bag, cut in ½-inch slices and serve with Fried Chicken (Ajam Goreng Asem) (*see index*), Bean Sprout Dish (Gado-Gado Penganten) (*see index*), and Grated Coconut with Dried Shrimp (Bubuk Buras) (*see index*).

CHAPTER 19

GENERAL RECIPES

In this chapter will be found methods for preparing food items commonly used in many recipes.

COCONUT BUTTER

Grate meat from a fresh coconut and toast in an ungreased skillet until golden brown and crisp. Grind twice, until it becomes a soft butter. If put in a tightly covered jar and refrigerated, can be kept for several weeks.

FRIED CRISP ONION FLAKES

Quarter onions, then cut in paper thin slices and fry in vegetable oil until crisp and golden brown. In a tightly covered jar, can be kept for several weeks. Fresh onions can be replaced by the dehydrated onion flakes available at local markets. Before use, these onion flakes should be fried in hot oil until crisp and light brown.

FRIED SOYBEANS

Used as a garnish. Wash one cup of soybeans, drain and deep fry in oil over moderate heat for 15 minutes, or until golden brown. Drain on absorbent paper. In a tightly covered jar, these can be kept for several weeks.

OMELET SLICES

Used as a garnish for many dishes. Put two tablespoons of beaten egg in a skillet greased with a few drops of oil. Tip the skillet in order to let egg spread over the bottom, then cook over moderate heat until light brown underneath. Omelet is rolled and cut into 1/8-inch slices.

ROASTED SHRIMP PASTE

Place a tablespoon of shrimp paste* in aluminum foil. Roast in a moderate (350°) oven for 15 minutes. Remove and grind.

SLICED GINGER

Fresh ginger root is used most frequently in fish, seafood, meat and poultry dishes. Only a few slices of fresh ginger root are required to create the desired taste-effect.

To slice ginger, scrape the skin off a 1-inch piece of ginger, wash, and cut into ⅛-inch slices. When "a slice of ginger" is required, it is one of these.

TAMARIND JUICE

To make one cup of tamarind juice, soak 2 tablespoons of shelled tamarind in 1 cup of water for 30 minutes. Stir until dissolved. Sieve. Can be kept for several days in the refrigerator.

CHAPTER 20

COOKING GLOSSARY

Terms Used in Cookery

BAKE: to cook by dry heat, especially in an oven.

BAKING POWDER: a leavening agent used in baking.

BARBECUE: to roast meat on spit or rock over coals, or under broiler heat, usually basting with a highly seasoned sauce.

BASTE: to moisten meat or other food while cooking, to add flavor and prevent drying of surface.

BEAT: to blend by mixing thoroughly.

BLANCH: to parboil, or pour boiling water over, a food, then drain it with cold water. Used to remove skins from peanuts, almonds, etc.

BLEND: to mix two or more ingredients until well combined.

BOIL: to cook in rapidly moving liquid, in which bubbles appear to surface and break.

BRAISE: to cook slowly in a covered utensil in a small amount of liquid or in steam, on top of range or in oven.

BROIL: to cook directly under heat or over open fire or grill.

CONDIMENTS: food seasonings, such as salt, pepper, herbs, spices, and relishes.

CUT: There are several methods of cutting: *diagonal slicing,* used in Chinese and Indonesian cooking for slicing stalk-like vegetables, such as Chinese cabbage and carrots, so that a large cut area will be exposed to the heat in cooking and in absorbing flavors; *straight slicing* is used for meats and fleshy and fibrous vegetables like mushrooms, scallions, etc. (meat is cut against the grain, at right angles to the direction of the fibers, and into slices).

DEEP FRY: to cook in a deep layer of fat.

FRY: to cook in a small amount of fat, also called sauté or panfry.

GARNISH: to decorate.

GRILL: *see* broil.

JULIENNE: designating foodstuffs cut in matchlike strips.

KNEAD: to work and press dough with the hands, at the same time folding and stretching.

MARINATE: to soak in vinegar, lemon juice, etc.

PANFRY: to cook in a small amount of fat.

PARBOIL: to boil in water only until partially cooked.

POACH: to cook gently in hot liquid so that shape of food is retained.

ROAST: to cook by dry heat, usually uncovered, especially in the oven.

SAUTÉ: to fry in a small amount of fat.

SEASON: to add seasonings, such as salt and pepper.

SIMMER: to cook in liquid below boiling point.

STEW: to cook slowly, in a small amount of liquid, for a long time.

STIR: to mix ingredients with a circular motion.

STOCK: the liquid resulting from the cooking of meat, fish, or vegetables.

WHIP: to beat rapidly to incorporate air, as in egg, cream, and gelatin mixtures.

Oven Temperature[*]

250°–300° = slow
300°–325° = slow moderate
350°–375° = moderate
400°–425° = hot
450°–475° = very hot
500°–525° = extremely hot

Tables of Weights and Measures

3 teaspoons = 1 tablespoon
16 tablespoons = 1 cup
1 cup = ½ pint
2 cups = 1 pint
2 pints = 1 quart
16 ounces = 1 pound
1 fluid ounce = 2 tablespoons
16 fluid ounces = 1 pint

[*] Degrees Fahrenheit.

Miscellaneous Measures

Butter (approximate measures):
4 sticks (1 pound) = 2 cups
1 stick (¼ pound) = ½ cup
½ stick (⅛ pound) = ¼ cup

Eggs (whole):
1 medium = ¼ cup
2 medium = ⅓–½ cup
3 medium = ½–⅔ cup
4 medium = ⅔–1 cup

Contents of cans:

Size	Average contents
8 oz.	= 1 cup
picnic	= 1¼ cups
No. 300	= 1¾ cups
No. 303	= 2 cups
No. 2	= 2½ cups
No. 2½	= 3½ cups
No. 3	= 5¾ cups
No. 10	= 12–13 cups

Syrup:
very thin syrup = ½ cup sugar to 2 cups water
thin syrup   = 1 cup sugar to 2 cups water
medium syrup = 1½ cups sugar to 2 cups water
heavy syrup   = 2 cups sugar to 2 cups water

Lemon:
1 lemon, juice of = about 2 or 3 tablespoons

Indonesian Cookery Terms

abon fried shredded meat
ajam chicken
amandel almond
anjang a special kind of dish
asam tamarind, sour
atjar pickles

babat tripe
babi pork
bakar roast
bakso meat balls
baktjang stuffed rice wrapped in banana leaves
bandrek gingered syrup
basa wet, fresh
bawang onion
babek duck
belada peppered
beras rice
biasa plain, common
bidji stone
bifstik beefsteak
bihun rice sticks
bubuk powder
bubur porridge
bumbu spices
buntjies green beans
buntut tail
buras rice wrapped in banana leaves

dadar omelet
daging meat
dandang steamer

dendeng crisp meat
djagung corn
djahe ginger
djamur kuping cloud ears
djuhie squid
duku Indonesian fruit
durian Indonesian fruit

ebbi, udang kering dried shrimp
empal fried meat
es ice

gembung swell
goreng fry
gulai dish
gulung roll

hati heart

ikan fish
isi filled, stuffed

jotjio kidney

kambing goat
kastanje chestnut
katjang kapri snow peas
katjang kedele soybeans
katjang merah red kidney beans
katjang tanah peanut
kelapa, kopior coconut
kentang potato

kepiting crab
kerie curry
ketimun cucumber
kodok frog
koek cake, cookie
kol cabbage
krenten raisins
kuah sauce
kue cake
kukus steam
kukusan steamer
kuning yellow

lada, lombok hot red pepper
lada mudah, lombok hidjau
  hot green pepper
lambok fresh, soft, wet
lapis layer
lida tongue
lobak white radish
lontong rice wrapped in
  banana leaves

mangistan Indonesian fruit
manis sweet
masak cook
merah red
mie noodles
misoa Chinese noodles

nasi rice

obi, ubi sweet potato
otak brain

padai, pedes hot
pakai use
pandjang long
panggang grill, roast
pangsit wonton
perkedel meat balls,
  soft fritters
perut stomach
petis shrimp sauce
petjel mixed salad
petjili chutney
pisang banana
putih white

rabu lung
rambutan fruit
rebung bamboo shoot
rebus boil
rempejek fritter
rudjak fruit salad

sagu tapioca flour
sajur vegetables
sambal condiment
santan coconut milk
saos sauce
sarang burung bird's-nest
sate skewered meat
sawi white cabbage,
  Chinese cabbage
sawoh Indonesian fruit
selada air lettuce
semoor smothered
setrup syrup

so-un, laksa shining noodles,
  cellophane noodles
spek bacon
spek koek layer cake
sop soup
soto soup

tahu bean cake
taotjo salted soybeans
tauge, toge bean sprouts
telur egg
tepung flour
terasi shrimp paste
terong eggplant
tim steam
tiram oyster

tito pork tripe
tjempedak Indonesian fruit
tjendol beverage
tjha sauté
tjuka vinegar
tomat tomato
tulang bone
tumis sauté

udang shrimp
urap mixed salad

wadjid rice cookie
widjen sesame seed
wortel carrot

INDEX

Index · **247**